RESUMES FOR

HEALTH AND MEDICAL CAREERS

FOURTH EDITION

RESUMES FOR
HEALTH AND MEDICAL
CAREERS

The Editors of McGraw-Hill

New York   Chicago   San Francisco   Lisbon   London   Madrid   Mexico City
Milan   New Delhi   San Juan   Seoul   Singapore   Sydney   Toronto

The McGraw·Hill Companies

Library of Congress Cataloging-in-Publication Data

Camenson, Blythe.
    Resumes for health and medical careers. — 4th ed. / by Blythe Camenson.
        p.   cm.
    Rev. ed. of: Resumes for health and medical careers / the editors of VGM
Career Books. 3rd ed. c2004.
      ISBN-13: 978-0-07-154535-8 (alk. paper)
      ISBN-10: 0-07-154535-2 (alk. paper)
      1. Résumés (Employment)   2. Medical personnel—Vocational guidance.
3. Cover letters.   I. Title.
[DNLM: 1. Health Occupations.   2. Job Application.   W 21 C181r 2008]

    R690.R48   2008
    610.69—dc22   2008022933

2 3 4 5 6 7 8 9 10 11 12 13 14 15 16 17 18 19 20 21 QPD/QPD 0 9

ISBN 978-0-07-154535-8
MHID   0-07-154535-2

McGraw-Hill books are available at special quantity discounts to use as premiums and
sales promotions or for use in corporate training programs. To contact a representative,
please visit the Contact Us pages at www.mhprofessional.com.

This book is printed on acid-free paper.

Contents

Introduction

Your resume is a piece of paper (or an electronic document) that serves to introduce you to the people who will eventually hire you. To write a thoughtful resume, you must thoroughly assess your personality, your accomplishments, and the skills you have acquired. The act of composing and submitting a resume also requires you to carefully consider the company or individual that might hire you. What are they looking for, and how can you meet their needs? This book shows you how to organize your personal information and experience into a concise and well-written resume, so that your qualifications and potential as an employee will be understood easily and quickly by a complete stranger.

Writing the resume is just one step in what can be a daunting job search process, but it is an important element in the chain of events that will lead you to your new position. While you are probably a talented, bright, and charming person, your resume may not reflect these qualities. A poorly written resume can get you nowhere; a well-written resume can land you an interview and potentially a job. A good resume can even lead the interviewer to ask you questions that will allow you to talk about your strengths and highlight the skills you can bring to a prospective employer. Even a person with very little experience can find a good job if he or she is assisted by a thoughtful and polished resume.

Lengthy, typewritten resumes are a thing of the past. Today, employers do not have the time or the patience for verbose documents; they look for tightly composed, straightforward, action-based resumes. Although a one-page resume is the norm, a two-page resume may be warranted if you have had extensive job experience or have changed careers and truly need the space to properly position yourself. If, after careful editing, you still need more than one page to present yourself, it's acceptable to use a second page. A crowded resume that's hard to read would be the worst of your choices.

Distilling your work experience, education, and interests into such a small space requires preparation and thought. This book takes you step-by-step through the process of crafting an effective resume that will stand out in today's competitive marketplace. It serves as a workbook and a place to write down your experiences, while also including the techniques you'll need to pull all the necessary elements together. In the following pages, you'll find many examples of resumes that are specific to your area of interest. Study them for inspiration and find what appeals to you. There are a variety of ways to organize and present your information; inside, you'll find several that will be suitable to your needs. Good luck landing the job of your dreams.

The Elements of an Effective Resume

An effective resume is composed of information that employers are most interested in knowing about a prospective job applicant. This information is conveyed by a few essential elements. The following is a list of elements that are found in most resumes—some essential, some optional. Later in this chapter, we will further examine the role of each of these elements in the makeup of your resume.

- Heading
- Objective and/or Keyword Section
- Work Experience
- Education
- Honors
- Activities
- Certificates and Licenses
- Publications
- Professional Memberships
- Special Skills
- Personal Information
- References

The first step in preparing your resume is to gather information about yourself and your past accomplishments. Later you will refine this information, rewrite it using effective language, and organize it into an attractive layout. But first, let's take a look at each of these important elements individually so you can judge their appropriateness for your resume.

Heading

Although the heading may seem to be the simplest section of your resume, be careful not to take it lightly. It is the first section your prospective employer will see, and it contains the information she or he will need to contact you. At the very least, the heading must contain your name, your home address, and, of course, a phone number where you can be reached easily.

In today's high-tech world, many of us have multiple ways that we can be contacted. You may list your e-mail address if you are reasonably sure the employer makes use of this form of communication. Keep in mind, however, that others may have access to your e-mail messages if you send them from an account provided by your current company. If this is a concern, do not list your work e-mail address on your resume. If you are able to take calls at your current place of business, you should include your work number, because most employers will attempt to contact you during typical business hours.

If you have voice mail or a reliable answering machine at home or at work, list its number in the heading and make sure your greeting is professional and clear. Always include at least one phone number in your heading, even if it is a temporary number, where a prospective employer can leave a message.

You might have a dozen different ways to be contacted, but you do not need to list all of them. Confine your numbers or addresses to those that are the easiest for the prospective employer to use and the simplest for you to retrieve.

Objective

When seeking a specific career path, it is important to list a job or career objective on your resume. This statement helps employers know the direction you see yourself taking, so they can determine whether your goals are in line with those of their organization and the position available. Normally, an objective is one to two sentences long. Its contents will vary depending on your career field, goals, and personality. The objective can be specific or general, but it should always be to the point. See the sample resumes in this book for examples.

If you are planning to use this resume online, or you suspect your potential employer is likely to scan your resume, you will want to include a "keyword" in the objective. This allows a prospective employer, searching hundreds of resumes for a specific skill or position objective, to locate the keyword and find your resume. In essence, a keyword is what's "hot" in your particular field at a given time. It's a buzzword, a shorthand way of getting a particular message across at a glance. For example, if you are a lawyer, your objective might state your desire to work in the area of corporate litigation. In this case, someone searching for the keyword "corporate litigation" will pull up your resume and know that you want to plan, research, and present cases at trial on behalf of the corporation. If your objective states that you "desire a challenging position in systems design," the keyword is "systems design," an industry-specific shorthand way of saying that you want to be involved in assessing the need for, acquiring, and implementing high-technology systems. These are keywords and every industry has them, so it's becoming more and more important to include a few in your resume. (You may need to conduct additional research to make sure you know what keywords are most likely to be used in your desired industry, profession, or situation.)

There are many resume and job-search sites online. Like most things in the online world, they vary a great deal in quality. Use your discretion. If you plan to apply for jobs online or advertise your availability this way, you will want to design a scannable resume. This type of resume uses a format that can be easily scanned into a computer and added to a database. Scanning allows a prospective employer to use keywords to quickly review each applicant's experience and skills, and (in the event that there are many candidates for the job) to keep your resume for future reference.

Many people find that it is worthwhile to create two or more versions of their basic resume. You may want an intricately designed resume on high-quality paper to mail or hand out *and* a resume that is designed to be scanned into a computer and saved on a database or an online job site. You can even create a resume in ASCII text to e-mail to prospective employers. For further information, you may wish to refer to the *Guide to Internet Job Searching*, by Frances Roehm and Margaret Dikel, updated and published every other year by McGraw-Hill. This excellent book contains helpful and detailed information about formatting a resume for Internet use. To get you started, in Chapter 3 we have included a list of things to keep in mind when creating electronic resumes.

Although it is usually a good idea to include an objective, in some cases this element is not necessary. The goal of the objective statement is to provide the employer with an idea of where you see yourself going in the field. However, if you are uncertain of the exact nature of the job you seek, including an objective that is too specific could result in your not being considered for a host of perfectly acceptable positions. If you decide not to use an objective heading in your resume, you should definitely incorporate the information that would be conveyed in the objective into your cover letter.

Work Experience

Work experience is arguably the most important element of them all. Unless you are a recent graduate or former homemaker with little or no relevant work experience, your current and former positions will provide the central focus of the resume. You will want this section to be as complete and carefully constructed as possible. By thoroughly examining your work experience, you can get to the heart of your accomplishments and present them in a way that demonstrates and highlights your qualifications.

If you are just entering the workforce, your resume will probably focus on your education, but you should also include information on your work or volunteer experiences. Although you will have less information about work experience than a person who has held multiple positions or is advanced in his or her career, the amount of information is not what is most important in this section. How the information is presented and what it says about you as a worker and a person are what really count.

As you create this section of your resume, remember the need for accuracy. Include all the necessary information about each of your jobs, including your job title, dates of employment, name of your employer, city, state, responsibilities, special projects you handled, and accomplishments. Be sure to list only accomplishments for which you were directly responsible. And don't be alarmed if you haven't participated in or worked on special projects, because this section may not be relevant to certain jobs.

The most common way to list your work experience is in *reverse chronological order*. In other words, start with your most recent job and work your way backward. This way, your prospective employer sees your current (and often most important) position before considering your past employment. Your most recent position, if it's the most important in terms of responsibilities and relevance to the job for which you are applying, should also be the one that includes the most information as compared to your previous positions.

Even if the work itself seems unrelated to your proposed career path, you should list any job or experience that will help sell your talents. If you were promoted or given greater responsibilities or commendations, be sure to mention the fact.

The following worksheet is provided to help you organize your experiences in the working world. It will also serve as an excellent resource to refer to when updating your resume in the future.

WORK EXPERIENCE

Job One:

Job Title _____

Dates _____

Employer _____

City, State _____

Major Duties _____

_____

_____

_____

_____

_____

_____

_____

_____

Special Projects _____

_____

_____

_____

Accomplishments _____

_____

_____

_____

_____

_____

Job Two:

Job Title _____

Dates _____

Employer _____

City, State _____

Major Duties _____

_____

_____

_____

_____

_____

_____

_____

Special Projects _____

_____

_____

_____

Accomplishments _____

_____

_____

_____

_____

_____

_____

Job Three:

Job Title _____

Dates _____

Employer _____

City, State _____

Major Duties _____

_____

_____

_____

_____

_____

_____

_____

Special Projects _____

_____

_____

_____

Accomplishments _____

_____

_____

_____

_____

_____

_____

_____

Job Four:

Job Title _____

Dates _____

Employer _____

City, State _____

Major Duties _____

_____

_____

_____

_____

_____

_____

_____

Special Projects _____

_____

_____

_____

Accomplishments _____

_____

_____

_____

_____

_____

_____

Education

Education is usually the second most important element of a resume. Your educational background is often a deciding factor in an employer's decision to interview you. Highlight your accomplishments in school as much as you did those accomplishments at work. If you are looking for your first professional job, your education or life experience will be your greatest asset because your related work experience will be minimal. In this case, the education section becomes the most important means of selling yourself.

Include in this section all the degrees or certificates you have received; your major or area of concentration; all of the honors you earned; and any relevant activities you participated in, organized, or chaired. Again, list your most recent schooling first. If you have completed graduate-level work, begin with that and work your way back through your undergraduate education. If you have completed college, you generally should not list your high-school experience; do so only if you earned special honors, you had a grade point average that was much better than the norm, or this was your highest level of education.

If you have completed a large number of credit hours in a subject that may be relevant to the position you are seeking but did not obtain a degree, you may wish to list the hours or classes you completed. Keep in mind, however, that you may be asked to explain why you did not finish the program. If you are currently in school, list the degree, certificate, or license you expect to obtain and the projected date of completion.

The following worksheet will help you gather the information you need for this section of your resume.

EDUCATION

School One _____

Major or Area of Concentration _____

Degree _____

Dates _____

School Two _____

Major or Area of Concentration _____

Degree _____

Dates _____

Honors

If you include an honors section in your resume, you should highlight any awards, honors, or memberships in honorary societies that you have received. (You may also incorporate this information into your education section.) Often, the honors are academic in nature, but this section also may be used for special achievements in sports, clubs, or other school activities. Always include the name of the organization awarding the honor and the date(s) received. Use the following worksheet to help you gather your information.

HONORS

Honor One _____

Awarding Organization _____

Date(s) _____

Honor Two _____

Awarding Organization _____

Date(s) _____

Honor Three _____

Awarding Organization _____

Date(s) _____

Honor Four _____

Awarding Organization _____

Date(s) _____

Honor Five _____

Awarding Organization _____

Date(s) _____

Activities

Perhaps you have been active in different organizations or clubs; often an employer will look at such involvement as evidence of initiative, dedication, and good social skills. Examples of your ability to take a leading role in a group should be included on a resume, if you can provide them. The activities section of your resume should present neighborhood and community activities, volunteer positions, and so forth. In general, you may want to avoid listing any organization whose name indicates the race, creed, sex, age, marital status, sexual orientation, or nation of origin of its members because this could expose you to discrimination. Use the following worksheet to list the specifics of your activities.

ACTIVITIES

Organization/Activity _____

Accomplishments _____

_____

_____

Organization/Activity _____

Accomplishments _____

_____

_____

Organization/Activity _____

Accomplishments _____

_____

_____

As your work experience grows through the years, your school activities and honors will carry less weight and be emphasized less in your resume. Eventually, you will probably list only your degree and any major honors received. As time goes by, your job performance and the experience you've gained become the most important elements in your resume, which should change to reflect this.

Certificates and Licenses

If your chosen career path requires specialized training, you may already have certificates or licenses. You should list these if the job you are seeking requires them and you, of course, have acquired them. If you have applied for a license but have not yet received it, use the phrase "application pending."

License requirements vary by state. If you have moved or are planning to relocate to another state, check with that state's board or licensing agency for all licensing requirements.

Always make sure that all of the information you list is completely accurate. Locate copies of your certificates and licenses, and check the exact date and name of the accrediting agency. Use the following worksheet to organize the necessary information.

CERTIFICATES AND LICENSES

Name of License _____

Licensing Agency _____

Date Issued _____

Name of License _____

Licensing Agency _____

Date Issued _____

Name of License _____

Licensing Agency _____

Date Issued _____

Publications

Some professions strongly encourage or even require that you publish. If you have written, coauthored, or edited any books, articles, professional papers, or works of a similar nature that pertain to your field, you will definitely want to include this element. Remember to list the date of publication and the publisher's name, and specify whether you were the sole author or a coauthor. Book, magazine, or journal titles are generally italicized, while the titles of articles within a larger publication appear in quotes. (Check with your reference librarian for more about the appropriate way to present this information.) For scientific or research papers, you will need to give the date, place, and audience to whom the paper was presented.

Use the following worksheet to help you gather the necessary information about your publications.

PUBLICATIONS

Title and Type (Note, Article, etc.) _____

Title of Publication (Journal, Book, etc.) _____

Publisher _____

Date Published _____

Title and Type (Note, Article, etc.) _____

Title of Publication (Journal, Book, etc.) _____

Publisher _____

Date Published _____

Title and Type (Note, Article, etc.) _____

Title of Publication (Journal, Book, etc.) _____

Publisher _____

Date Published _____

Professional Memberships

Another potential element in your resume is a section listing professional memberships. Use this section to describe your involvement in professional associations, unions, and similar organizations. It is to your advantage to list any professional memberships that pertain to the job you are seeking. Many employers see your membership as representative of your desire to stay up-to-date and connected in your field. Include the dates of your involvement and whether you took part in any special activities or held any offices within the organization. Use the following worksheet to organize your information.

PROFESSIONAL MEMBERSHIPS

Name of Organization _____

Office(s) Held_____

Activities _____

Dates _____

Name of Organization _____

Office(s) Held_____

Activities _____

Dates _____

Name of Organization _____

Office(s) Held_____

Activities _____

Dates _____

Name of Organization _____

Office(s) Held_____

Activities _____

Dates _____

Special Skills

The special skills section of your resume is the place to mention any special abilities you have that relate to the job you are seeking. You can use this element to present certain talents or experiences that are not necessarily a part of your education or work experience. Common examples include fluency in a foreign language, extensive travel abroad, or knowledge of a particular computer application. "Special skills" can encompass a wide range of talents, and this section can be used creatively. However, for each skill you list, you should be able to describe how it would be a direct asset in the type of work you're seeking because employers may ask just that in an interview. If you can't think of a way to do this, it may be extraneous information.

Personal Information

Some people include personal information on their resumes. This is generally not recommended, but you might wish to include it if you think that something in your personal life, such as a hobby or talent, has some bearing on the position you are seeking. This type of information is often referred to at the beginning of an interview, when it may be used as an icebreaker. Of course, personal information regarding your age, marital status, race, religion, or sexual orientation should never appear on your resume as personal information. It should be given only in the context of memberships and activities, and only when doing so would not expose you to discrimination.

References

References are not usually given on the resume itself, but a prospective employer needs to know that you have references who may be contacted if necessary. All you need to include is a single sentence at the end of the resume: "References are available upon request," or even simply, "References available." Have a reference list ready—your interviewer may ask to see it! Contact each person on the list ahead of time to see whether it is all right for you to use him or her as a reference. This way, the person has a chance to think about what to say *before* the call occurs. This helps ensure that you will obtain the best reference possible.

Chapter 2

Writing Your Resume

Now that you have gathered the information for each section of your resume, it's time to write it out in a way that will get the attention of the reviewer—hopefully, your future employer! The language you use in your resume will affect its success, so you must be careful and conscientious. Translate the facts you have gathered into the active, precise language of resume writing. You will be aiming for a resume that keeps the reader's interest and highlights your accomplishments in a concise and effective way.

Resume writing is unlike any other form of writing. Although your seventh-grade composition teacher would not approve, the rules of punctuation and sentence building are often completely ignored. Instead, you should try for a functional, direct writing style that focuses on the use of verbs and other words that imply action on your part. Writing with action words and strong verbs characterizes you to potential employers as an energetic, active person, someone who completes tasks and achieves results from his or her work. Resumes that do not make use of action words can sound passive and stale. These resumes are not effective and do not get the attention of any employer, no matter how qualified the applicant. Choose words that display your strengths and demonstrate your initiative. The following list of commonly used verbs will help you create a strong resume:

administered	assembled
advised	assumed responsibility
analyzed	billed
arranged	built

carried out	inspected
channeled	interviewed
collected	introduced
communicated	invented
compiled	maintained
completed	managed
conducted	met with
contacted	motivated
contracted	negotiated
coordinated	operated
counseled	orchestrated
created	ordered
cut	organized
designed	oversaw
determined	performed
developed	planned
directed	prepared
dispatched	presented
distributed	produced
documented	programmed
edited	published
established	purchased
expanded	recommended
functioned as	recorded
gathered	reduced
handled	referred
hired	represented
implemented	researched
improved	reviewed

saved	supervised
screened	taught
served as	tested
served on	trained
sold	typed
suggested	wrote

Let's look at two examples that differ only in their writing style. The first resume section is ineffective because it does not use action words to accent the applicant's work experiences.

WORK EXPERIENCE
Regional Sales Manager

Manager of sales representatives from seven states. Manager of twelve food chain accounts in the East. In charge of the sales force's planned selling toward specific goals. Supervisor and trainer of new sales representatives. Consulting for customers in the areas of inventory management and quality control.

Special Projects: Coordinator and sponsor of annual Food Industry Seminar.

Accomplishments: Monthly regional volume went up 25 percent during my tenure while, at the same time, a proper sales/cost ratio was maintained. Customer-company relations were improved.

In the following paragraph, we have rewritten the same section using action words. Notice how the tone has changed. It now sounds stronger and more active. This person accomplished goals and really *did* things.

WORK EXPERIENCE
Regional Sales Manager

Managed sales representatives from seven states. Oversaw twelve food chain accounts in the eastern United States. Directed the sales force in planned selling toward specific goals. Supervised and trained new sales representatives. Counseled customers in the areas of inventory management and quality control. Coordinated and sponsored the annual Food Industry Seminar. Increased monthly regional volume by 25 percent and helped to improve customer-company relations during my tenure.

One helpful way to construct the work experience section is to make use of your actual job descriptions—the written duties and expectations your employers have for a person in your current or former position. Job descriptions are rarely written in proper resume language, so you will have to rework them, but they do include much of the information necessary to create this section of your resume. If you have access to job descriptions for your former positions, you can use the details to construct an action-oriented paragraph. Often, your human resources department can provide a job description for your current position.

The following is an example of a typical human resources job description, followed by a rewritten version of the same description employing action words and specific details about the job. Again, pay attention to the style of writing instead of the content, as the details of your own experience will be unique.

WORK EXPERIENCE
Public Administrator I

Responsibilities: Coordinate and direct public services to meet the needs of the nation, state, or community. Analyze problems; work with special committees and public agencies; recommend solutions to governing bodies.

Aptitudes and Skills: Ability to relate to and communicate with people; solve complex problems through analysis; plan, organize, and implement policies and programs. Knowledge of political systems, financial management, personnel administration, program evaluation, and organizational theory.

WORK EXPERIENCE
Public Administrator I

Wrote pamphlets and conducted discussion groups to inform citizens of legislative processes and consumer issues. Organized and supervised 25 interviewers. Trained interviewers in effective communication skills.

After you have written out your resume, you are ready to begin the next important step: assembly and layout.

Chapter 3

Assembly and Layout

At this point, you've gathered all the necessary information for your resume and rewritten it in language that will impress your potential employers. Your next step is to assemble the sections in a logical order and lay them out on the page neatly and attractively to achieve the desired effect: getting the interview.

Assembly

The order of the elements in a resume makes a difference in its overall effect. Clearly, you would not want to bury your name and address somewhere in the middle of the resume. Nor would you want to lead with a less important section, such as special skills. Put the elements in an order that stresses your most important accomplishments and the things that will be most appealing to your potential employer. For example, if you are new to the workforce, you will want the reviewer to read about your education and life skills before any part-time jobs you may have held for short durations. On the other hand, if you have been gainfully employed for several years and currently hold an important position in your company, you should list your work accomplishments ahead of your educational information, which has become less pertinent with time.

Certain things should always be included in your resume, but others are optional. The following list shows you which are which. You might want to use it as a checklist to be certain that you have included all of the necessary information.

Essential	Optional
Name	Cellular Phone Number
Address	Pager Number
Phone Number	E-Mail Address or Website Address
Work Experience	
Education	Voice Mail Number
References Phrase	Job Objective
	Honors
	Special Skills
	Publications
	Professional Memberships
	Activities
	Certificates and Licenses
	Personal Information
	Graphics
	Photograph

Your choice of optional sections depends on your own background and employment needs. Always use information that will put you in a favorable light—unless it's absolutely essential, avoid anything that will prompt the interviewer to ask questions about your weaknesses or something else that could be unflattering. Make sure your information is accurate and truthful. If your honors are impressive, include them in the resume. If your activities in school demonstrate talents that are necessary for the job you are seeking, allow space for a section on activities. If you are applying for a position that requires ornamental illustration, you may want to include border illustrations or graphics that demonstrate your talents in this area. If you are answering an advertisement for a job that requires certain physical traits, a photo of yourself might be appropriate. A person applying for a job as a computer programmer would *not* include a photo as part of his or her resume. Each resume is unique, just as each person is unique.

Types of Resumes

So far we have focused on the most common type of resume—the *reverse chronological* resume—in which your most recent job is listed first. This is the type of resume usually preferred by those who have to read a large number of resumes, and it is by far the most popular and widely circulated. However, this style of presentation may not be the most effective way to highlight *your* skills and accomplishments.

For example, if you are reentering the workforce after many years or are trying to change career fields, the *functional* resume may work best. This type of resume puts the focus on your achievements instead of the sequence of your work history. In the functional resume, your experience is presented through your general accomplishments and the skills you have developed in your working life.

A functional resume is assembled from the same information you gathered in Chapter 1. The main difference lies in how you organize the information. Essentially, the work experience section is divided in two, with your job duties and accomplishments constituting one section and your employers' names, cities, and states; your positions; and the dates employed making up the other. Place the first section near the top of your resume, just below your job objective (if used), and call it *Accomplishments* or *Achievements*. The second section, containing the bare essentials of your work history, should come after the accomplishments section and can be called *Employment History*, since it is a chronological overview of your former jobs.

The other sections of your resume remain the same. The work experience section is the only one affected in the functional format. By placing the section that focuses on your achievements at the beginning, you draw attention to these achievements. This puts less emphasis on where you worked and when, and more on what you did and what you are capable of doing.

If you are changing careers, the emphasis on skills and achievements is important. The identities of previous employers (who aren't part of your new career field) need to be downplayed. A functional resume can help accomplish this task. If you are reentering the workforce after a long absence, a functional resume is the obvious choice. And if you lack full-time work experience, you will need to draw attention away from this fact and put the focus on your skills and abilities. You may need to highlight your volunteer activities and part-time work. Education may also play a more important role in your resume.

The type of resume that is right for you will depend on your personal circumstances. It may be helpful to create both types and then compare them. Which one presents you in the best light? Examples of both types of resumes are included in this book. Use the sample resumes in Chapter 5 to help you decide on the content, presentation, and look of your own resume.

Resume or Curriculum Vitae?

A curriculum vitae (CV) is a longer, more detailed synopsis of your professional history that generally runs three or more pages in length. It includes a summary of your educational and academic background as well as teaching and research experience, publications, presentations, awards, honors, affiliations, and other details. Because the purpose of the CV is different from that of the resume, many of the rules we've discussed thus far involving style and length do not apply.

A curriculum vitae is used primarily for admissions applications to graduate or professional schools, independent consulting in a variety of settings, proposals for fellowships or grants, or applications for positions in academia. As with a resume, you may need different versions of a CV for different types of positions. You should only send a CV when one is specifically requested by an employer or institution.

Like a resume, your CV should include your name, contact information, education, skills, and experience. In addition to the basics, a CV includes research and teaching experience, publications, grants and fellowships, professional associations and licenses, awards, and other information relevant to the position for which you are applying. You can follow the advice presented thus far to gather and organize your personal information.

Special Tips for Electronic Resumes

Because there are many details to consider in writing a resume that will be posted or transmitted on the Internet, or one that will be scanned into a computer when it is received, we suggest that you refer to the *Guide to Internet Job Searching*, by Frances Roehm and Margaret Dikel, as previously mentioned. However, here are some brief, general guidelines to follow if you expect your resume to be scanned into a computer.

- Use standard fonts in which none of the letters touch.

- Keep in mind that underlining, italics, and fancy scripts may not scan well.

- Use boldface and capitalization to set off elements. Again, make sure letters don't touch. Leave at least a quarter inch between lines of type.

- Keep information and elements at the left margin. Centering, columns, and even indenting may change when the resume is optically scanned.

- Do not use any lines, boxes, or graphics.

- Place the most important information at the top of the first page. If you use two pages, put "Page 1 of 2" at the bottom of the first page and put your name and "Page 2 of 2" at the top of the second page.

- List each telephone number on its own line in the header.

- Use multiple keywords or synonyms for what you do to make sure your qualifications will be picked up if a prospective employer is searching for them. Use nouns that are keywords for your profession.

- Be descriptive in your titles. For example, don't just use "assistant"; use "legal office assistant."

- Make sure the contrast between print and paper is good. Use a high-quality laser printer and white or very light colored 8½-by-11-inch paper.

- Mail a high-quality laser print or an excellent copy. Do not fold or use staples, as this might interfere with scanning. You may, however, use paper clips.

In addition to creating a resume that works well for scanning, you may want to have a resume that can be e-mailed to reviewers. Because you may not know what word processing application the recipient uses, the best format to use is ASCII text. (ASCII stands for "American Standard Code for Information Interchange.") It allows people with very different software platforms to exchange and understand information. (E-mail operates on this principle.) ASCII is a simple, text-only language, which means you can include only simple text. There can be no use of boldface, italics, or even paragraph indentations.

To create an ASCII resume, just use your normal word processing program; when finished, save it as a "text only" document. You will find this option under the "save" or "save as" command. Here is a list of things to *avoid* when crafting your electronic resume:

- Tabs. Use your space bar. Tabs will not work.

- Any special characters, such as mathematical symbols.

- Word wrap. Use hard returns (the return key) to make line breaks.

- Centering or other formatting. Align everything at the left margin.

- Bold or italic fonts. Everything will be converted to plain text when you save the file as a "text only" document.

Check carefully for any mistakes before you save the document as a text file. Spellcheck and proofread it several times; then ask someone with a keen eye to go over it again for you. Remember: the key is to keep it simple. Any attempt to make this resume pretty or decorative may result in a resume that is confusing and hard to read. After you have saved the document, you can cut and paste it into an e-mail or onto a website.

Layout for a Paper Resume

A great deal of care—and much more formatting—is necessary to achieve an attractive layout for your paper resume. There is no single appropriate layout that applies to every resume, but there are a few basic rules to follow in putting your resume on paper:

- Leave a comfortable margin on the sides, top, and bottom of the page (usually one to one and a half inches).

- Use appropriate spacing between the sections (two to three line spaces are usually adequate).

- Be consistent in the *type* of headings you use for different sections of your resume. For example, if you capitalize the heading EMPLOYMENT HISTORY, don't use initial capitals and underlining for a section of equal importance, such as Education.

- Do not use more than one font in your resume. Stay consistent by choosing a font that is fairly standard and easy to read, and don't change it for different sections. Beware of the tendency to try to make your resume original by choosing fancy type styles; your resume may end up looking unprofessional instead of creative. Unless you are in a very creative and artistic field, you should almost always stick with tried-and-true type styles like Times New Roman and Palatino, which are often used in business writing. In the area of resume styles, conservative is usually the best way to go.

CHRONOLOGICAL RESUME

Patricia Allen, RRA

645 Green Street • Nashville, TN 37214 • (615) 555-8765 • P.Allen@xxx.com

Work History

2003–Present • Vanderbilt Children's Hospital, Nashville, TN

Medical Records Administrator

• Analyze patient data for processing insurance requests and hospital care programs.

• Supervise medical records clerks and transcriptionists.

• Implemented new system for retrieving medical records.

• Developed in-service program for medical records clerks.

• Developed policies for processing insurance requests.

• Evaluated hospital medical records system.

2002–2003

Nashville General Hospital at Meharry, Nashville, TN

Medical Records Administrator

• Assisted staff in evaluating efficiency of patient medical care.

• Analyzed patient health care programs.

• Supervised all medical records clerks.

Education

1998–2002 • Vanderbilt University, Nashville, TN

Bachelor of Science in Medical Records Administration

Courses

• Anatomy
• Medical Law
• Medical Records Administration
• Computer Science
• Statistics
• Medical Terminology
• Disease Classification

Certification

Registered Records Administrator, 2002

References Available Upon Request

FUNCTIONAL RESUME

LESLIE SUNGENTUK

4812 Burlington Drive • Cocoa, FL 32927 • (321) 555-1052 • sungentuk@xxx.com

OVERVIEW
- Retired from United States Marine Corps in February 2001
- Currently employed as certified prosthetist, manager, and part-time consultant
- Experience in design, manufacturing, and service of prosthetic components
- Assist prosthetic clinics with patient evaluation, management, and prosthetic care

EMPLOYMENT
Spectrum Artificial Limb Corporation • *May 2001 to Present*
Manager, Prosthetic Design and Service Division

Veterans Administration Medical Center • *September 2004 to Present*
Management Consultant

Veterans Memorial Hospital • *March 2005 to Present*
Patient Management Consultant

PROSTHETIC EDUCATION
Northwestern University, School of Prosthetics, Chicago, Illinois
Courses: • Below-Knee Prosthetics for Prosthetists
• Above-Knee Prosthetics for Prosthetists
• Upper-Extremity Prosthetics for Prosthetists
• Review Course in Prosthetics
• Immediate Post-Surgical Fitting for Prosthetists

University of California, UCLA Extension, Los Angeles, CA
Course: • Suction Below Knee Prosthetics

PROSTHETIC CERTIFICATION
- American Board Certification: October 9, 1995
- Qualified Prosthetist: May 15, 1990—License #555

INDUSTRIAL TRAINING
Otto Bock Orthopedic Industry, Inc., Minneapolis, Minnesota
Course: Lower Extremity Modular System

Motion Control, Salt Lake City, Utah
Course: Fitting Procedures of the Utah Artificial Arm

Durr-Fillauer Medical, Inc., Chattanooga, Tennessee
Course: Scandinavian Flexible Socket

IPOS, Niagara Falls, New York
Course: Flexible Socket Fabrication

Otto Bock Orthopedic Industry, Inc., Minneapolis, Minnesota
Courses: Myoelectrically Controlled Upper Extremity System and System MYOBOCK

Flex-Foot, Inc., Irving, California
Course: Basic Flex-Foot

REFERENCES AVAILABLE UPON REQUEST

- Always try to fit your resume on one page. If you are having trouble with this, you may be trying to say too much. Edit out any repetitive or unnecessary information, and shorten descriptions of earlier jobs where possible. Ask a friend you trust for feedback on what seems unnecessary or unimportant. For example, you may have included too many optional sections. Today, with the prevalence of the personal computer as a tool, there is no excuse for a poorly laid out resume. Experiment with variations until you are pleased with the result.

Remember that a resume is not an autobiography. Too much information will only get in the way. The more compact your resume, the easier it will be to review. If a person who is swamped with resumes looks at yours, catches the main points, and then calls you for an interview to fill in some of the details, your resume has already accomplished its task. A clear and concise resume makes for a happy reader and a good impression.

There are times when, despite extensive editing, the resume simply cannot fit on one page. In this case, the resume should be laid out on two pages in such a way that neither clarity nor appearance is compromised. Each page of a two-page resume should be marked clearly: the first should indicate "Page 1 of 2," and the second should include your name and the page number, for example, "Julia Ramirez—Page 2 of 2." The pages should then be paper-clipped together. You may use a smaller type size (in the same font as the body of your resume) for the page numbers. Place them at the bottom of page one and the top of page two. Again, spend the time now to experiment with the layout until you find one that looks good to you.

Always show your final layout to other people and ask them what they like or dislike about it, and what impresses them most when they read your resume. Make sure that their responses are the same as what you want to elicit from your prospective employer. If they aren't the same, you should continue to make changes until the necessary information is emphasized.

Proofreading

After you have finished typing the master copy of your resume and before you have it copied or printed, thoroughly check it for typing and spelling errors. Do not place all your trust in your computer's spellcheck function. Use an old editing trick and read the whole resume backward—start at the end and read it right to left and bottom to top. This can help you see the small errors or inconsistencies that are easy to overlook. Take time to do it right because a single error on a document this important can cause the reader to judge your attention to detail in a harsh light.

Have several people look at the finished resume just in case you've missed an error. Don't try to take a shortcut; not having an unbiased set of eyes examine your resume now could mean embarrassment later. Even experienced editors can easily overlook their own errors. Be thorough and conscientious with your proofreading so your first impression is a perfect one.

We have included the following rules of capitalization and punctuation to assist you in the final stage of creating your resume. Remember that resumes often require use of a shorthand style of writing that may include sentences without periods and other stylistic choices that break the standard rules of grammar. Be consistent in each section and throughout the whole resume with your choices.

RULES OF CAPITALIZATION

- Capitalize proper nouns, such as names of schools, colleges, and universities; names of companies; and brand names of products.

- Capitalize major words in the names and titles of books, tests, and articles that appear in the body of your resume.

- Capitalize words in major section headings of your resume.

- Do not capitalize words just because they seem important.

- When in doubt, consult a style manual such as *Words into Type* (Prentice Hall) or *The Chicago Manual of Style* (The University of Chicago Press). Your local library can help you locate these and other reference books. Many computer programs also have grammar help sections.

RULES OF PUNCTUATION

- Use commas to separate words in a series.

- Use a semicolon to separate series of words that already include commas within the series. (For an example, see the first rule of capitalization.)

- Use a semicolon to separate independent clauses that are not joined by a conjunction.

- Use a period to end a sentence.

- Use a colon to show that examples or details follow that will expand or amplify the preceding phrase.

- Avoid the use of dashes.

- Avoid the use of brackets.

- If you use any punctuation in an unusual way in your resume, be consistent in its use.

- Whenever you are uncertain, consult a style manual.

Putting Your Resume in Print

You will need to buy high-quality paper for your printer before you print your finished resume. Regular office paper is not good enough for resumes; the reviewer will probably think it looks flimsy and cheap. Go to an office supply store or copy shop and select a high-quality bond paper that will make a good first impression. Select colors like white, off-white, or possibly a light gray. In some industries, a pastel may be acceptable, but be sure the color and feel of the paper make a subtle, positive statement about you. Nothing in the choice of paper should be loud or unprofessional.

If your computer printer does not reproduce your resume properly and produces smudged or stuttered type, either ask to borrow a friend's or take your disk (or a clean original) to a printer or copy shop for high-quality copying. If you anticipate needing a large number of copies, taking your resume to a copy shop or a printer is probably the best choice.

Hold a sheet of your unprinted bond paper up to the light. If it has a watermark, you will want to point this out to the person helping you with copies; the printing should be done so that the reader can read the print and see the watermark the right way up. Check each copy for smudges or streaks. This is the time to be a perfectionist—the results of your careful preparation will be well worth it.

Chapter 4

The Cover Letter

Once your resume has been assembled, laid out, and printed to your satisfaction, the next and final step before distribution is to write your cover letter. Though there may be instances where you deliver your resume in person, you will usually send it through the mail or online. Resumes sent through the mail always need an accompanying letter that briefly introduces you and your resume. The purpose of the cover letter is to get a potential employer to read your resume, just as the purpose of the resume is to get that same potential employer to call you for an interview.

Like your resume, your cover letter should be clean, neat, and direct. A cover letter usually includes the following information:

1. Your name and address (unless it already appears on your personal letterhead) and your phone number(s); see item 7.

2. The date.

3. The name and address of the person and company to whom you are sending your resume.

4. The salutation ("Dear Mr." or "Dear Ms." followed by the person's last name, or "To Whom It May Concern" if you are answering a blind ad).

5. An opening paragraph explaining why you are writing (for example, in response to an ad, as a follow-up to a previous meeting, at the suggestion of someone you both know) and indicating that you are interested in whatever job is being offered.

6. One or more paragraphs that tell why you want to work for the company and what qualifications and experiences you can bring to the position. This is a good place to mention some detail about

that particular company that makes you want to work for them; this shows that you have done some research before applying.

7. A final paragraph that closes the letter and invites the reviewer to contact you for an interview. This can be a good place to tell the potential employer which method would be best to use when contacting you. Be sure to give the correct phone number and a good time to reach you, if that is important. You may mention here that your references are available upon request.

8. The closing ("Sincerely" or "Yours truly") followed by your signature in a dark ink, with your name typed under it.

Your cover letter should include all of this information and be no longer than one page in length. The language used should be polite, businesslike, and to the point. Don't attempt to tell your life story in the cover letter; a long and cluttered letter will serve only to annoy the reader. Remember that you need to mention only a few of your accomplishments and skills in the cover letter. The rest of your information is available in your resume. If your cover letter is a success, your resume will be read and all pertinent information reviewed by your prospective employer.

Producing the Cover Letter

Cover letters should always be individualized because they are always written to specific individuals and companies. Never use a form letter for your cover letter or copy it as you would a resume. Each cover letter should be unique, and as personal and lively as possible. (Of course, once you have written and rewritten your first cover letter until you are satisfied with it, you can certainly use similar wording in subsequent letters. You may want to save a template on your computer for future reference.) Keep a hard copy of each cover letter so you know exactly what you wrote in each one.

There are sample cover letters in Chapter 6. Use them as models or for ideas of how to assemble and lay out your own cover letters. Remember that every letter is unique and depends on the particular circumstances of the individual writing it and the job for which he or she is applying.

After you have written your cover letter, proofread it as thoroughly as you did your resume. Again, spelling or punctuation errors are a sure sign of carelessness, and you don't want that to be a part of your first impression on a prospective employer. This is no time to trust your spellcheck function. Even after going through a spelling and grammar check, your cover letter should be carefully proofread by at least one other person.

Print the cover letter on the same quality bond paper you used for your resume. Remember to sign it, using a good dark-ink pen. Handle the letter and resume carefully to avoid smudging or wrinkling, and mail them together in an appropriately sized envelope. Many stores sell matching envelopes to coordinate with your choice of bond paper.

Keep an accurate record of all resumes you send out and the results of each mailing. This record can be kept on your computer, in a calendar or notebook, or on file cards. Knowing when a resume is likely to have been received will keep you on track as you make follow-up phone calls.

About a week after mailing resumes and cover letters to potential employers, contact them by telephone. Confirm that your resume arrived and ask whether an interview might be possible. Be sure to record the name of the person you spoke to and any other information you gleaned from the conversation. It is wise to treat the person answering the phone with a great deal of respect; sometimes the assistant or receptionist has the ear of the person doing the hiring.

You should make a great impression with the strong, straightforward resume and personalized cover letter you have just created. We wish you every success in securing the career of your dreams!

Chapter 5

Sample Resumes

This chapter contains dozens of sample resumes for people pursuing a wide variety of jobs and careers.

There are many different styles of resumes in terms of graphic layout and presentation of information. These samples represent people with varying amounts of education and experience. Use them as models for your own resume. Choose one resume or borrow elements from several different resumes to help you construct your own.

Franklin Wu

5391 Southward Plaza   (510) 555-9008

Walnut Creek, CA 94596   Frank.Wu@xxx.com

Job Objective

To obtain a position as a management optician in a fast-paced retail store

Education

Graduated Hayward Community College, Hayward, CA

June 2007

Graduated North Central High School, Chicago, IL

June 2005

Work Experience

Great Spectacles, Walnut Creek, CA

Management Optician, 2007–present

Valley Vision, Pleasanton, CA

Sales Associate, 2005–2006

Special Skills

• Excellent customer service skills

• Fashion styling experience

• Knowledge of adjustment, repair, and fitting of glasses and contact lenses

Certification

American Board of Optometry Certificate, 2007

Seminars

Cal-Q Optics to prepare for licensing, 2007

Opti-Fair (annual three-day seminar)

References

Available on request

JANE R. REYNOLDS

1241 Rue Louis XVI
Montreal, Quebec 42T 3T1 Canada
Cellular: 514-555-1926
E-mail: Jane.Reynolds@xxx.com

Secondary School/University

• Concordia University, Montreal, Quebec, 2004 to 2008
• St. Brides' High School, 2000 to 2004

Examinations Achieved

• Certificate of SYS Chemistry, grade A, 2004
• English, Mathematics, Biology, Chemistry, grade B, 2004

Grades in Pharmacy B.Sc. Courses

• Pharmaceutical Chemistry, 83 percent
• Pharmaceutics, 97 percent
• Pharmacy Practice, 84 percent
• Drugs and Disease, 90 percent
• Drug Disposition and Biopharmaceutics, 84 percent

Employment

Dispenser
Summer Employment, 2005, 2006, and 2007
Robert G. Gross, M.R.Pharm.S.

References

Available on Request

Ishtar Edwan

5024 Orinda Lane • Huntsville, AL 35804 • (205) 555-9601 • iedwan@xxx.com

Goal

To be a dental hygienist in a family practice

Education

Faulkner University, Montgomery, AL—Associate Degree in Dental Hygiene, 2000
Cathedral High School—Honors Diploma, 1998

Employment

Hygienist, 2004 to present
Robert Reynolds, D.D.S.
8629 Weber Street
Huntsville, AL 35804

- Examine teeth and gums
- Clean and polish teeth
- Take and develop x-rays
- Screen patients for oral cancer
- Give fluoride treatments
- Instruct patients in home oral health procedures

Dental Assistant and Hygienist, 1999 to 2004
Amanda Lindsay, D.D.S.
4825 Ridge Road
Montgomery, AL 36109

- Took and developed x-rays
- Made preliminary impressions for study casts
- Participated in "four-hand" procedures
- Prepared filling materials and cements
- Took impressions
- Kept the patients comfortable

References

Available on request

PATRICIA WHITE

987 West 44th Street • Cheyenne, WY 82001 • (307) 555-9872 • PKWhite@xxx.com

PROFESSIONAL OBJECTIVE

To obtain a position that offers an opportunity to demonstrate superior managerial ability and administrative decision-making skills in a nursing home environment

SUMMARY OF QUALIFICATIONS

- High degree of motivation
- Ability and patience to train and develop office/professional staff
- Thorough knowledge of Microsoft Office, including Word, PowerPoint, and Excel
- Dictation

EDUCATION

University of Wyoming, B.A. Business
Laramie, Wyoming
2003

EXPERIENCE

Assistant Director
Longview Manor, Cheyenne, WY
April 2006–present

Business Manager
Mountain Top Nursing Home, Cheyenne, WY
October 2003–April 2006

REFERENCES

Excellent professional and personal references are available upon request

Hanna Mayers, M.D.

Home Address   Work Address
111 Barclay St.   Henry Wilkins Hospital
Cincinnati, OH 45219   2799 North Street
HannaMayers@xxx.com   Cincinnati, OH 45219
513-555-7987   513-555-8811

Specialty
Neonatology

Education
M.D., Wayne State University Medical School, Dayton, OH
1998–2002

M.B.A. with concentration on finance, Indiana University, Bloomington, IN
1992–1993
Graduated magna cum laude

B.S., Notre Dame University, South Bend, IN
1988–1992
Graduated magna cum laude

Medical Training
Fellow, Neonatal Intensive Care Unit
Henry Wilkins Hospital, Cincinnati, OH
2005–present
Program Director: James Minor, M.D.

- Participate in this comprehensive program encompassing all phases of
  neonatal care, including intensive care unit, step-down unit, and well-baby
  nurseries
- Expect to have performed approximately 220 cranial ultrasounds, 30 EEGs,
  and 150 umbilical catheter placements upon completion

Residency, Department of Medicine
Memorial Hospital, Denver, CO
2002–2005
Program Director: Robert Jackson, M.D.

Medical Training *continued*

- 650-bed tertiary care facility
- Worked in inpatient and ambulatory medicine, including extensive ICU, CCU, oncology, and emergency room experience
- Performed multiple procedures, including central line placement, lumbar puncture, bone marrow biopsy, and ventilator management

Business Experience

General Motors Company, Casting Division
Dearborn, MI
Financial and Profits Analysis
June 1996–July 1998

General Motors Company, Casting Plant
Indianapolis, IN
Accounting and Financial Analysis
August 1992–May 1996

Certifications

- Advanced Cardiac Life Support Certification, 2004
- Basic Cardiac Life Support Certification, 2003
- American Board of Internal Medicine, 2002

Professional Societies

- American Medical Association
- American College of Physicians
- American Pediatric Society
- American Academy of Pediatrics

Licensure

State of Ohio, 2005
State of Colorado, 2004

References

Furnished upon request

ROBERTO VASQUEZ

85 Starview Lane • Kalamazoo, MI 49002
Home: (616) 555-6812 • Cellular: (616) 555-3448
E-mail: R.Vasquez@xxx.com

CAREER OBJECTIVE

Position as a health care administrator in a hospital or clinic serving the
mentally handicapped

EDUCATION

Bachelor of Science, June 2000
Psychology Major, Accounting Minor
Ball State University, Muncie, Indiana

• 3.49 G.P.A.
• Kappa Delta Tau (Honor Society in Psychology)
• Dean's List (five times)

PROFESSIONAL EXPERIENCE

Managing Director, Craig L. Turner Clinic
January 2007–present
• Responsible for all aspects of clinic operation including financial planning,
  personnel, and cost control
• Coordinate all nursing and medical activities

Assistant Director, Kelly Hospital
June 2004–December 2006
• Managed medical record department, inpatient admittance, and budget
  planning

Administrative Supervisor, Muncie Community Hospitals
July 2000–May 2004
• Trained personnel, hired staff, and administered educational services

REFERENCES AVAILABLE

Omar J. Jaksa

642 Brady Road • Westfield, NJ 07901 • Omar.Jaksa@xxx.com • 451-555-2886

Education

University of Texas at Austin
Degree: B.S. in Biology, 1998

URWAR Medical School, Santa Anna, D.R.
Degree: M.D., 2001

Postgraduate Training

Transitional Internship, July 2001–June 2002
Frankford Hospital, Troy, PA

Residency, July 2002–June 2005
Presbyterian University, Troy, PA

Nephrology Fellowship, June 2005–present
Mt. Sinai Medical Center, New York, NY

Examinations & Licensures

• FMGMS passed in July 2000 (ECFMG License #55555555)
• FLEX passed in June 2001
• DEA License #MD-55555-L in April 2003
• PA State License #555555 in April 2005
• Internal Medicine Board passed in August 2005 (License #555555)

Memberships

• Alpha Epsilon Delta
• American College of Physicians
• American Medical Association
• Renal Physicians Association
• The National Kidney Foundation

Background

• Volunteer Nurse's Aide in Austin, 1995
• Volunteer Physician Assistant in Austin, October 1996–August 1998
• Fluent in English, Spanish, French, and Arabic

References

Available on request

GRAHAM T. BOOKER

Safety Instruction • Environmental Assessment • Safety Management

2354 Fuller Place, Apt. 2C • Indianapolis, IN 46250

317-555-7896

graham.booker@xxx.com

EDUCATION

Bachelor of Science, 2002

Major: Health and Safety Education

Indiana State University, Terre Haute, Indiana

Relevant Courses:

- Personal Health Science
- Health Biostatistics
- Human Anatomy
- Health Services
- Individual Safety
- Health and Safety Education
- Human Ecology
- Epidemiology
- Community Health
- Sociology

EXPERIENCE

Indiana Army National Guard, Shelbyville, Indiana
2004–present
Company Executive Officer

- Coordinated command service support requirements.
- Responsible for all logistics.
- Counseled and performed annual evaluations for personnel.
- Solicited suggestions for procedural improvements.
- Conducted all physical fitness training.
- Appointed as Company Safety Officer—planned and managed safety classes.
- Representative in the Indiana National Guard Safety Council.
- Appointed Unit Marshal—enforced military justice at the company level.

AGA Fleet Products, Indianapolis, Indiana
2002–2004
Distribution Services Clerk

- Filled all orders.
- Coordinated all departments and their needs.

EXPERIENCE *continued*

- Provided support to the company president.
- Developed and maintained databases.

Indiana State University Department of Recreation, Terre Haute, Indiana
2000–2002, Summers
Lifeguard

- Oversaw the safety of all individuals in the pool area.
- Improved and implemented safety procedures.
- Trained new lifeguards.
- Completed cardiopulmonary resuscitation and emergency first aid course.

MILITARY SERVICE

- Completed Army helicopter flight school training, November 2005.
- Served as First Lieutenant in the Indiana National Guard.
- Received Air Crewman's Badge, Army Service Ribbon, and the Army Commendation Medal.
- Completed Officer Candidate School while a full-time college student.

REFERENCES AVAILABLE UPON REQUEST

SHAWNA JONES

133 Lincoln Drive

Detroit, MI 48099

(613) 555-3361

E-mail: sjones@xxx.com

POSITION DESIRED

Health Care Administrator in a hospital or clinic.

EXPERIENCE

Director, Vicksburg Community Hospitals
1996 to present

Responsible for all aspects of hospital operation, including financial planning, personnel, medical activities, and facilities management.

Assistant Director, Vicksburg Community Hospitals
1995 to 1996

Handled inpatient and outpatient admittance, cost control, and emergency services.

Assistant Director, Plainwell Community Hospitals
1992 to 1995

Managed billing practices, cost control, and new cost procedures.

EDUCATION

Western Michigan University, Kalamazoo, Michigan
M.S., Public Health Administration, May 1996
B.S., Business with Biology Minor, May 1992

Participated in professional in-service seminars on fiscal and health care issues including cost control, financial planning, billing and collection systems, inpatient admittance, and Lynn Hall's lecture series relating occupational therapy to the hospital environment.

COMMUNITY SERVICE

Volunteer firefighter in Vicksburg for eight years.
Member of the committee to study emergency care facilities in Vicksburg.
Member of the American Public Health Association and the American Academy of Hospital Administrators.

REFERENCES

Available upon request

ANNETTE KEITH

555 Leavitt Drive, Apartment 2 • Yonkers, NY 10710

Annette.Keith@xxx.com • (914) 555-6892

PROFESSIONAL EXPERIENCE

July 2007 to June 2008
Fellowship in Gynecology at Albert College of Medicine, Bronx,
New York

July 2004 to June 2007
Residency in Internal Medicine at New York Hospital, Queens,
New York
Affiliated with New York Hospital, Cornell University, Ithaca,
New York

May 2000 to October 2003
Medical Officer, Brazil, South America

October 1998 to April 2000
Postgraduate Resident at Kayo Medical College Hospital,
Kayo, Mexico

April 1997 to April 1998
Rotating Internship at the Queens Hospital, Queens Medical College,
and Queens University, Bronx, New York

CERTIFYING EXAMINATIONS

- Eligible to appear for the American Board of Obstetrics and
  Gynecology Examination, June 2008
- Diplomate of the American Board of Internal Medicine,
  September 2007
- FLEX exam, New York State, December 2004. Grades 83 percent
  and 86 percent
- FMGEMS exam, January 2003. Grade 85 percent

Page 1 of 2

EDUCATION

September 1992 to August 1998
Bachelor of Medicine and Bachelor of Surgery (M.B.B.S.)
Queens Medical College, Bronx, New York

June 1990 to March 1992
Premedical course at The National College
Queens University, Bronx, New York

LICENSES

New York State, #555555
July 2007

Mexico, #5555
May 1998

AWARDS AND HONORS

Medical
Class of 110 students
- 1st rank in first M.B.B.S. exam
- 1st rank in second M.B.B.S. exam
- 12th rank in final M.B.B.S. exam

Premedical
State-level examination
- 4th rank in first year
- 11th rank in second year

MEMBERSHIPS

Member of the American College of Physicians

REFERENCES

Available on request

Eve Fujimora

4366 South Street

San Francisco, CA 94101

Phone: (415) 555-9698

E-mail: Eve.Fujimora@xxx.com

Career Goal

To obtain a position teaching dental hygiene

Education

University of California, San Francisco
M.S. Dental Hygiene, 2005

Southwestern College, San Diego, CA
B.S. Dental Hygiene, 2003

Work Experience

Instructor of Dental Hygiene, June 2005–present
University of California, San Francisco
Classes: Oral Anatomy, Periodontology and Physiology

Graduate Assistant, September 2003–May 2005
University of California, San Francisco
Duties: teaching section in Periodontology and Physiology, grading
assignments and quizzes, and recording attendance for lecture periods

References

Available upon request

PABLO SANCHEZ

786 Zelda Street • Dallas, TX 75201 • Pablo.Sanchez@xxx.com • (214) 555-2299

OBJECTIVE

To obtain employment in a health care environment where I can apply my knowledge of education and exercise my analytical and interpersonal skills.

EDUCATION

Bachelor of Science with Honors in Education

University of Texas at Dallas, May 2005

Grade Point Average: 3.3 out of 4.0

EXPERIENCE

Educational Attendant, June 2005–Present
Tri-West Services for Mental Health, Dallas, TX
• Involved in one-on-one contact with patients on the unit taking vital signs, directing recreational activities, and completing rounds.
• Responsible for charting individual patients and providing assessments of patients' physical and mental status.

Reformat Editor, February 2004–May 2005
Valley, Inc., Dallas, TX
• Member of a four-person team that reformatted Valley's All Lines Service (covering insurance agent/agency licensing) from a word processing format into a database format.

Research Assistant, August 2003–May 2005
Department of Science, University of Texas at Dallas
• Assisted in scoring, coding, analyzing, and interpreting data in various research areas.

Computer Lab Assistant, August 2001–May 2005
University of Texas at Dallas
• Assisted students with all aspects of Macintosh usage.
• Issued and set up university e-mail accounts.

SPECIAL SKILLS

I have worked with Macintosh computers extensively. I am also familiar with all aspects of Delta Graph and Excel. In addition, I have experience with two statistical packages, GAUSS and SPSS, and I learn new software packages quickly.

ACTIVITIES

• Member of the Phi Delta Theta Fraternity
• Alumni secretary, Fall 2003
• Pledge committee member, Fall 2002
• Intramural softball
• Member of the Education Club, Spring 2004–Present
• Peer academic advisor, Fall 2004

REFERENCES

Available upon request

DARREN C. HANOVER 405 D Lane, Apartment 3C • Providence, RI 02777
E-mail: dhanover@xxx.com • Cellular: (401) 555-8907

POSITION SOUGHT
Pediatric Nurse Practitioner

EDUCATION
Pediatric Nurse Practitioner
St. Joseph's School of Nursing—Providence, RI
Certificate as Pediatric Nurse Practitioner, 2001

Department of Postgraduate Medicine and Health Professional Education
St. Joseph's School of Nursing—Providence, RI
Pediatric Emergency Nursing, 2005

Seventh Annual Nursing Conference on Pediatric Primary Care
The PNP in the Changing Health Care System
National Association of Pediatric Nurse Associates and Practitioners—
San Diego, CA • 2006

Graduate
St. Joseph's School of Nursing—Providence, RI
Master of Science in Nursing, 2000

Undergraduate
Medical College of Georgia—Augusta, GA
Bachelor of Science in Nursing, 1996

PROFESSIONAL CREDENTIALS
RN License
Rhode Island: #55555555 Exp. 10/31/2008
New York: #55555555 Exp. 10/31/2009

Pediatric Nurse Practitioner
Certificate, St. Joseph's School of Nursing
The National Board of Pediatric Nurse Practitioners and Associates Certification, 2001
Pediatric Nurse Practitioner, ID #55555555

PROFESSIONAL EXPERIENCE
Hawley Community Hospital Clinic—Providence, RI
Pediatric Nurse Practitioner
February 2003 to present
• Act as primary care nurse in the Pediatric and Well-Baby Clinic.
• Plan and develop methods, practices, and approaches pertinent to health maintenance
  of pediatric patients (birth to 18 years) and their families.

PROFESSIONAL EXPERIENCE *continued*
- Carry out a complete range of pediatric health services including assessing status of patients, evaluating the effectiveness of care, and initiating or modifying treatment. This involves counseling, teaching, coordinating services, networking with other disciplines, developing new techniques, and establishing and revising criteria for care.
- Act as clinical instructor and preceptor for graduate PNP students, RN students, and medical screening students planning and executing in-services.
- Responsible, as pediatric nursing consultant for the hospital, for planning and conducting parenting classes and serving as a member of the Community Health Education Committee.

Ireland Community Hospital—Louisville, KY
Pediatric Nurse Practitioner
July 2001 to February 2003
- Same duties as at Hawley Community Hospital Clinic, above.
- In addition, responsible for all admission and discharge physicals on normal newborns, including ordering required studies and managing specific abnormalities. Gave all newborn prenatal and postnatal classes.
- Rotated as weekend hospital nursing supervisor.
- Served on the Audit and Community Health Education Committee.

Tripler Medical Center—Providence, RI
Clinical Head Nurse
July 1999 to July 2001
- In charge of 33-bed pediatric medical-surgical ward caring for children requiring minimal to intensive care.
- Responsible for the administration and management of nursing activities on a busy pediatric ward through maximum utilization, evaluation, education, and training of nursing personnel.
- Supervised and was responsible for ten to twelve RNs and fifteen to twenty paraprofessionals and gave care to pediatric patients.
- As a clinical head nurse, responsible for assessing, planning, directing, giving, and evaluating nursing care.
- Served as hospital nursing supervisor one to two weekends per month and as maternal-child supervisor as needed.

PROFESSIONAL ORGANIZATIONS
National Association of Pediatric Nurse Associates and Practitioners • 2002 to present

National Association of Pediatric Nurse Associates and Practitioners—Rhode Island Chapter • 2004 to present

References available upon request or during interview.

MARK JONES

1031 116th St. • Fort Worth, TX 76102 • M.Jones@xxx.com • (817) 555-2310

OBJECTIVE

To utilize my professional abilities to obtain a position in the field of nursing.

EDUCATION

Lawrence Fire Department
EMT Defibulator
Texas State Certificate, 2007

University of Dallas–Fort Worth, Fort Worth, TX
General Studies, 34 semester hours, 2007

Gorgas Army Hospital, Fort Worth, TX
Enhanced Acute Trauma Certificate, 2004

Academy of Health Sciences, Fort Worth, TX
EMT/Medical Assistant Certificate, 2002

WORK EXPERIENCE

Gorgas Army Hospital, Fort Worth, TX
Pediatric Clinician, 2007–present
Nurse's Aide, 2005–2007
Medical Assistant/Phlebotomist, 2003–2005

U.S. Army; Fort Worth, TX, 5th/87th Infantry
Emergency Medical Technician, 2002–2003

AWARDS

Good Conduct Medal
U.S. Army, 2002 to 2005

REFERENCES

Available upon request

Pauline S. Birch

1610 Willow Lane • New Haven, KY 57220
(613) 555-1583 • P.Birch@xxx.com

Position Desired
School Psychologist

Education
Williamshire University (Online University)
Ed.S. School Psychology, 2007

Bellaire University (Online University)
M.A. Psychology, 2001

North Salem University (Online University)
B.A. Psychology, 1999

Certification
School Psychologist I

Work Experience
June 2006 to Present
Williamshire University
Counseling and Testing Clinic
Position: Part-Time Graduate Assistant

April 2003 to June 2006
Kramer Clinic
Position: Addictions Counselor

December 1999 to April 2001
Children's Services
Position: Counselor

Memberships
Student Representative, Graduate Council
Williamshire University

Vice President, Association of Graduate Counselors
Williamshire University

References
Available on request

THOMAS K. BODLE

555 Still Drive ▪ Saskatoon, Saskatchewan ▪ Canada S7J 4M7
Home: 232-555-4554 ▪ Work: 343-555-7680 ▪ E-mail: tbodle@xxx.com

CURRENT POSITION
Resident IV in Internal Medicine
Department of Medicine, The Queens Hospital
Saskatoon, Saskatchewan, Canada S7N 5M8
July 2007 to present

ACADEMIC QUALIFICATIONS
M.B.B.S., Indiana University, January 1992
M.D., Indiana University, September 1996
Postgraduate Specialty: Internal Medicine

Diploma, National Board of Medical Examinations, November 1999
Specialty: Nephrology

EXPERIENCE
January 2000–June 2002
Assistant Professor in Medicine
Department of Medicine, St. Mary's College & Hospital, Lafayette, IN

July 2002–June 2004
Two years of fellowship training in Nephrology, Division of Nephrology
Department of Internal Medicine, University of Queens Hospital, Alberta, Canada

July 2004–June 2007
Three years of core training in Internal Medicine
Department of Medicine, University of Queens Hospital, Alberta, Canada

AWARDS AND SCHOLARSHIPS
Resident research project won top prize for 2005–2006
Cyclosporin and Distal Renal Tubular Dysfunction in Renal Transplant Patients
Department of Medicine, University of Queens Hospital, Alberta, Canada

Social and Educational Scholarship of the Provincial Government
Awarded for five years, 1987–1991, while attending Indiana University

ADMINISTRATIVE POSTS
Administrative Resident, 2005
Department of Medicine, Valley Health Center
Alberta, Canada

Organizing Secretary, October 2001
Sixth Annual Conference of the Southern Chapter of Nephrology

ADMINISTRATIVE POSTS *continued*
Coordinator, 2000
Scientific Session, 15th Annual Conference of Nephrology

PROFESSIONAL EXPERIENCE
- Investigation, diagnosis, and management of all varieties of clinical nephrology problems.
- Hemodialysis (insertion of subclavian, jugular, femoral lines; creation of Scribner shunts; monitoring; and follow-up of patients on acute and chronic peritoneal dialysis).
- Peritoneal dialysis (insertion of acute peritoneal dialysis, monitoring, and follow-up of patients on acute and chronic peritoneal dialysis).
- Renal biopsies (300 adult biopsies, 75 transplant biopsies, and 30 pediatric biopsies).
- Live donor kidney perfusion (150 kidney perfusions).
- Renal transplant recipient monitoring and post-transplant follow-up, including evaluation of complications and management of rejection episodes (approximately 300 renal transplants).

TEACHING EXPERIENCE
- Theory classes in Internal Medicine and Nephrology for undergraduate students.
- Bedside clinical teaching for undergraduate and postgraduate students in Internal Medicine.
- Seminars, grand rounds, teaching rounds, journal club meetings.
- Classes for M.S. (nursing course) in Medicine.
- Classes for dialysis diploma students.

RESEARCH EXPERIENCE
I am interested in transplant immunology research and have completed one year of bench research studying the significance of anti-HLA Class I antibodies in renal transplant recipients and their role in the causation of rejection episodes. This work was supported by a grant from the Alberta Heritage Fund and was presented at the American Transplant Society annual meeting in 2004 and the American Society of Nephrology meeting in 2005.

MEMBERSHIPS
- Association of Physicians of America
- Southern Chapter, Society of Nephrology
- Medical Association of Canada

REFERENCES
Available on request

KEVIN E. CODY

5555 Field Avenue
Portland, OR 97786
Cellular: (503) 555-8976
E-mail: K.Cody@xxx.com

OBJECTIVE

Staff nurse anesthetist position with room for supervisory advancement within two years, in a modern, well-equipped, midsized medical facility where CRNAs and MDAs support each other while retaining their own autonomy.

SUMMARY OF QUALIFICATIONS

Clinical experience in small and large medical center settings, combining decision making with professional latitude. Experienced in all types of general and regional anesthesia with continuous epidural experience in postoperative pain relief. Possess strong interpersonal communication skills resulting in high degrees of patient satisfaction.

EDUCATION

Oregon Health and Science University, Portland, OR
Master of Arts in Health Services Management, 2007
University of Portland, Portland, OR
Bachelor of Science in Nursing, 2003

Oregon Health and Science University, Portland, OR
Diploma in Nurse Anesthesia, 2000

EXPERIENCE

Staff Anesthetist and Chief Anesthetist, Nurse Anesthesia Section • 2007 to present
Beaverton Community Hospital, Beaverton, OR
• Supervise and assume overall clinical and administrative responsibility for a
  two-anesthetist operating setting, averaging over 500 cases per year without the
  benefit of an assigned staff anesthesiologist.
• Serve as technical director and quality assurance coordinator for respiratory therapy
  services.
• Perform duties of Nursing Department chief in her absence.
• Administer clinical anesthesia with call coverage and provide continuous epidural
  postoperative pain management.

Staff Anesthetist and Assistant Supervisor, Nurse Anesthesia Section • 2005 to 2007
Brooke Medical Center, Portland, OR
• Provided relief supervision and assistance to CRNA staff and anesthesia residents
  administering anesthesia on complex surgical procedures.
• Assisted with anesthesia supplies and equipment ordering, maintenance, and evaluation.
• Served as a Basic Cardiac Life Support (BCLS) instructor for the anesthesia staff.
• Administered clinical anesthesia in medical center and Level I trauma center setting.

EXPERIENCE *continued*
Chief and Assistant Chief, Nurse Anesthesia Section • 2003 to 2005
Maywood Park Community Hospital, Maywood Park, OR
- Supervised staff of four CRNAs in operative setting averaging over 200 surgical cases per month.
- Managed anesthesia supply system, resulting in successful compliance with projected budgetary constraints.
- Converted daily anesthesia supply system to a daily cart exchange system to reduce time spent on daily restock.
- Administered clinical anesthesia with call coverage.

Staff Anesthetist and Clinical Instructor, Nurse Anesthesia Section • 2002 to 2003
Community Hospital, Gresham, OR
- Provided clinical supervision of Community Hospital, Phase II nurse anesthesia students.
- Designed a departmental continuing education program with approved credit by the American Association of Nurse Anesthetists (AANA). Developed a departmental quality assurance program.
- Administered clinical anesthesia with call coverage.

Staff Anesthetist, Nurse Anesthesia Section • 2000 to 2002
Memorial Hospital, Happy Valley, OR
- Developed departmental quality assurance program.
- Developed departmental continuing education program approved by the AANA.
- Developed a standardized anesthesia equipment setup for hospital-wide use in all CPR carts.
- Evaluated and gained approval for purchase of a new anesthesia gas mass spectrometry monitoring system.
- Administered clinical anesthesia with call coverage.

AFFILIATIONS
American Association of Nurse Anesthetists, member since 2000

LICENSURE AND CERTIFICATION
- Board of Nursing Examiners for the State of Oregon No. 55555555
- Council on Recertification of Nurse Anesthetists No. 55555

REFERENCES
Available on request

DAVID EDWARD GARCIA

17644 Ventura Blvd. • Los Angeles, CA 90024

Home: (213) 555-9876 • Cell: (213) 555-0036 • D.Garcia@xxx.com

- Registered medical laboratory technician
- Fluent in English and Spanish

EDUCATION

A.A., Riverside Junior College
Riverside, CA, 2001

EMPLOYMENT

Southern California Laboratories, Los Angeles, CA
August 2007–Present
Medical Laboratory Technician

U.C.L.A. Outpatient Clinic, Los Angeles, CA
June 2006–July 2007
Medical Laboratory Technician

Lowell Pharmaceuticals, Riverside, CA
May 2001–May 2006
Medical Laboratory Technician

MEMBERSHIPS

Internal Society for Clinical Laboratory Technology

REFERENCES

Available on request

Samuel Hong

9845 Corning Drive • Denver, CO 80233 • (303) 555-9347

Samuel.Hong@xxx.com

Objective

A position as ombudsman in a large teaching hospital

Education

Boston University, Boston, Massachusetts

M.S., Health Advocacy, 2004

Saint John's College, Annapolis, Maryland

B.A., Psychology, 1998

Experience

Boston HMO, Boston, Massachusetts, June 2004–Present

Individualize health care for patients and conduct sensitivity training sessions for staff members

St. John's Hospital, Annapolis, Maryland, June 2000–June 2004

Resolved problems and secured appropriate post-hospitalization services for patients, focusing on the elderly

Cambridge Nursing Center, Cambridge, Massachusetts, May 1998–June 2000

Acted on behalf of indigent patients

Additional Information

• Computer skills: Microsoft Office Suite 2000, including Word, Excel, Power-Point, and Access

• Foreign language: Chinese

Affiliations

• American Psychology Association

• National Society for Patient Representation and Consumer Affairs of the American Hospital Association

References

Available on request

PATRICK R. COLLEN

876 West Ninth Street • Little Rock, Arkansas 84542

Pat.Collen@xxx.com • (501) 555-9240

Objective

To gain a position in nutritional care.

Education

M.S. in Nutrition, 2007
University of Arkansas, Little Rock, AR

B.S. in Dietetics, 1998
University of Arkansas, Little Rock, AR

Experience

Dietary Director, 8/2007 to Present
St. Vincent North Rehab Hospital, Sherwood, AR
• Supervise in-depth nutritional assessment of patients on hyperalimentation.
• Supervise educational programs on weight reduction, diabetes, and geriatric nutrition.

Consultant Dietitian (part-time), 5/2004 to 8/2007
Veterans Hospital, Little Rock, AR
• Developed standards for nutritional care.

Clinical Dietitian, 4/1998 to 4/2004
St. Mary's Hospital, Cammack Village, AR
• Created cost-effective nourishment center.
• Established nutritional care standards for individuals with HIV, for use by local dietitians.

Skills

• Fluent in German, proficient in French
• Familiar with all relevant computer programs
• Excellent verbal communication skills
• Experienced public speaker

References available upon request

Alicia Alvarez

9867 Ashton Road
Lexington, KY 40506
a.alvarez@xxx.net
(606) 555-3494

Objective

To obtain a position as a respiratory therapist with a hospital interested in using my skills as a technical resource person. Prefer to move into management as department director.

Education

Bachelor's Degree in Respiratory Therapy, June 2005
Louisiana Tech Institute, Ruston, LA

Experience

Respiratory Therapist, April 2007–present
Lexington General Hospital, Lexington, KY
Supervised staff respiratory technicians and served as resource person for hospital staff.

Respiratory Therapist, August 2005–March 2007
Kentucky Clinic, Lexington, KY
Participated in the diagnosis, evaluation, and prevention of respiratory problems.

Additional Credentials

- Registered Respiratory Therapist
- Member, American Academy of Respiratory Therapists

References

Personal and professional references on request.

MARY ELLEN BOYD

65 Maple Drive • Medford, MA 02155 • (781) 555-9843 • Mary.Boyd@xxx.com

OBJECTIVE

To obtain a position as a respiratory therapist utilizing my experience in the long-term treatment of geriatric patients.

EDUCATION

Medford Technical School, Medford, MA
B.S., May 2006

COURSEWORK

- Biology I and II
- Chemistry I and II
- Physics
- Physiology
- Airway Management, Pharmacology
- Gas, Aerosol, and Humidity Therapy
- Pulmonary Rehabilitation
- Cardiopulmonary Anatomy
- Stress Analysis
- Software Engineering
- Mechanical Ventilation
- Ethics of Respiratory Therapy
- Systems and Disorders of Breathing

EXPERIENCE

Respiratory Therapist
May 2006–Present
Humana Hospital, Medford, MA
- Perform tests to evaluate and diagnose respiratory problems.
- Develop preoperative visitation program for surgical patients.
- Instruct patients in the use of respiratory treatment aids and methods.

REFERENCES

Available on request.

DAKSHISH KAPOOR

Present Address
765 Fifth Street
Washington, D.C. 20016
(202) 555-2213
D.Kapoor@xxx.com

Permanent Address
28 Octavia Terrace
Washington, D.C. 20019
(202) 555-9737

OBJECTIVE

Obtain a full-time position as a medical writer for a pharmaceutical company, medical school, textbook publisher, or government agency.

EDUCATION

Currently pursuing M.S. in technical writing with a concentration in biology.
Expected graduation date: May 2009
George Washington University, Washington, D.C.

B.S. with Highest Distinction in English, May 2006
American University, Washington, D.C.

EXPERIENCE

Summer Intern
Eli Lilly and Company, Indianapolis, IN
Summer 2007
• Analyzed new product data and prepared reports for use by in-house sales staff.
• Interviewed researchers and prepared articles for company publications.

Summer Intern
Washington Post, Washington, D.C.
Summer 2006
• Wrote columns on health fads, fitness, and new drugs.

CREDENTIALS

• Certificates from the American Medical Writers Association in pharmaceutical writing and editing
• Member, American Medical Writers Association
• Editor, *The Eagle*, American University college newspaper

REFERENCES AVAILABLE ON REQUEST

MICHAEL MARTINEZ
455 Lilac Lane
Lincoln, NE 68990
Martinez12@xxx.com
402-555-7892

EDUCATION
B.A. from University of Nebraska–Lincoln, 2005
• Magna Cum Laude, 3.93 G.P.A.
• Highest Departmental Honors in Chemistry, 4.0 G.P.A.
• All-American Football Lineman, Co-Captain in Senior Year
• Four Varsity Letters
• National Football Foundation and Hall of Fame Scholar-Athlete Award

M.D. from University of Nebraska Medical Center, Omaha, NE, 2008
• Honors Marks: Gross Anatomy and Systemic Pathology
• Clerkships in Pediatrics and Neuroscience

MILITARY EXPERIENCE
Second Lieutenant Medical Officer Training, 2005–2008
Corps—United States Army Reserve, Omaha National Guard

Omaha Medical Advisory Committee Member, 2007

WORK EXPERIENCE
Extern, Henry County Memorial Hospital
Omaha, NE, 2006–2007

Summer Research Intern, Methodist Sports Clinic
Lincoln, NE, 2006

RESEARCH EXPERIENCE
Senior Research Thesis in Department of Chemistry, University of
Nebraska, 2004–2005
Robert M. Gibbons, Ph.D.
Associate Professor of Chemistry

RESEARCH EXPERIENCE *continued*
Summer Research at St. Vincent's Sports Clinic, Lincoln, NE, 2003
Andrew M. Sporn, M.D.
Director of Research and Development

PUBLICATIONS
1. Gibbons, R. M., and M. Martinez. "Forward and Reverse Rate Constants in the Diel-Alder Reaction." Senior Research Thesis File, Duggan Library, University of Nebraska–Lincoln, May 2005.

2. Sporn, A., et al. "Isolated Fractures of the Tibial Eminence in Adults Associated with Anterior Laxity." *Journal of Sports Medicine*, Vol. 10, No. 1, Spring 2004.

MEDICAL ILLUSTRATIONS
1. Kingsman, M. A. "Neurovascular Injuries in the Wrists and Hands of Athletes," *Clinics in Sports Medicine*, Vol. 9, No. 2, April 2006.

2. Michaels, J. B., and M. E. Tory. "Meniscal Transplantation," Presentation, Duke University School of Medicine, Durham, North Carolina, May 2007.

REFERENCES
Available on request

Paula Thomas

974 Chestnut Hill Road • Newark, DE 19713

Paula_Thomas@xxx.com • (302) 555-9812

Qualifications

Ten years' experience in medical social work in a hospital environment as a certified social worker.

Education

Master's Degree in Social Work

University of Delaware

Newark, Delaware, 2005

Bachelor's Degree in Social Work

University of Delaware

Newark, Delaware, 2003

Diploma, Newark High School

Newark, Delaware, 1999

Rotary Exchange Student

Germany, 1997

Various A.C.S.W. Seminars

Work Experience

Leader of the Hospital Health Team

October 2006 to present

Atlantic Hospital, Newark, Delaware

Work Experience *continued*

- Coordinate the services of doctors, nurses, and other hospital health care professionals to ensure that all resources are employed in the recovery of individual patients.

Supervisor of the Pediatric Unit

June 2006 to October 2006

Atlantic Hospital, Newark, Delaware

- Helped ease fears of parents and children about patients' medical condition.
- Conducted family assessments.
- Referred parents to appropriate community services.

Community Health Services Coordinator

July 2003 to June 2006

Chocorus Community Hospital, Chocorus, New Hampshire

- Found homes for children without caretakers because of parental hospitalization.
- Helped elderly who needed nursing assistance in their own homes.
- Educated patients on health services available in community.
- Counseled patients on handling finances and family relationships changed by hospitalization.

Affiliations

- American Association of University Women
- Girls Club of Chocorus

References

Available upon request

Yuki Humachi

131 Palm Drive

Lawton, OK 73501

Yuki.Humachi@xxx.com

(580) 555-2232

SUMMARY

• Ten years' experience as a surgical technologist with a proven record of competence

• Solid background in supporting operating room team in military hospitals

• Excellent skills in planning and organizing operating room for a clean surgical environment

EDUCATION

Associate's Degree, Surgical Technology, 1997

Rochester Institute of Technology, Rochester, NY

CERTIFICATION

Certified Surgical Technologist

WORK EXPERIENCE

Surgical Technology Supervisor, 2001–Present

United States Army, Fort Sill Army Hospital

- Responsible for coordinating efforts of medical technologist, scrub technologist, and circulating surgical technologist

- Specialist in orthopedic procedures

Surgical Technologist, 1997–2001

Paxton Memorial Hospital

- Responsible for checking supplies and equipment; draping the sterile field; and operating EKG monitors, lights, and suction machines

REFERENCES

Available upon request

LESLIE SUNGENTUK

4812 Burlington Drive • Cocoa, FL 32927 • (321) 555-1052 • sungentuk@xxx.com

OVERVIEW
- Retired from United States Marine Corps in February 2001
- Currently employed as certified prosthetist, manager, and part-time consultant
- Experience in design, manufacturing, and service of prosthetic components
- Assist prosthetic clinics with patient evaluation, management, and prosthetic care

EMPLOYMENT
Spectrum Artificial Limb Corporation • *May 2001 to Present*
Manager, Prosthetic Design and Service Division

Veterans Administration Medical Center • *September 2004 to Present*
Management Consultant

Veterans Memorial Hospital • *March 2005 to Present*
Patient Management Consultant

PROSTHETIC EDUCATION
Northwestern University, School of Prosthetics, Chicago, Illinois
Courses:
- Below-Knee Prosthetics for Prosthetists
- Above-Knee Prosthetics for Prosthetists
- Upper-Extremity Prosthetics for Prosthetists
- Review Course in Prosthetics
- Immediate Post-Surgical Fitting for Prosthetists

University of California, UCLA Extension, Los Angeles, CA
Course: • Suction Below Knee Prosthetics

PROSTHETIC CERTIFICATION
- American Board Certification: October 9, 1995
- Qualified Prosthetist: May 15, 1990—License #555

INDUSTRIAL TRAINING
Otto Bock Orthopedic Industry, Inc., Minneapolis, Minnesota
Course: Lower Extremity Modular System

Motion Control, Salt Lake City, Utah
Course: Fitting Procedures of the Utah Artificial Arm

Durr-Fillauer Medical, Inc., Chattanooga, Tennessee
Course: Scandinavian Flexible Socket

IPOS, Niagara Falls, New York
Course: Flexible Socket Fabrication

Otto Bock Orthopedic Industry, Inc., Minneapolis, Minnesota
Courses: Myoelectrically Controlled Upper Extremity System and System MYOBOCK

Flex-Foot, Inc., Irving, California
Course: Basic Flex-Foot

REFERENCES AVAILABLE UPON REQUEST

Jill Nelson

Current Address:
897 Burlingame Ave.
Atlanta, GA 30319
(404) 555-9112

Permanent Address:
5311 Rosalind St., Apt. #3
Calumet City, IL 60409
(708) 555-9991

OBJECTIVE

Seeking an applied research and development position in the field of health care products.

EDUCATION

M.S., Materials Science & Marketing
Cornell University, Ithaca, NY
May 2007

B.S., Mechanical Engineering
University of California–Davis, Davis, CA
May 2005

EXPERIENCE

Research Assistant
• Investigated the micromechanical as well as the macromechanical properties of a ceramic matrix–ceramic fiber composite.
• Prepared testing specimens and performed various mechanical testing schemes, including three- and four-point bending and tensile test.

Lab Consultant
• Helped students debug programs written in Perl.

Research Assistant
• Investigated the possibility of two-polymer systems being the precursor of a superconducting material.
• Prepared various compositions of the polymer solutions and spun fibers via several methods.
• Carried out high-temperature mechanical testing to determine the survivability of the fiber under pyrolysis.

MEMBERSHIP

Student Chapter, American Society of Mechanical Engineers

REFERENCES AVAILABLE UPON REQUEST

KEKIE AKONI

1908 Ohana Street
Honolulu, HI 96825
Kekie.Akoni@xxx.com
(808) 555-9090

EDUCATION

B.S. Biomedical Engineering Technology, 2006
Chaminade University of Honolulu

EXPERIENCE

2006–Present
Whitehall and Miles, Inc.
Honolulu, HI

- Apply the principles and technologies of various disciplines to the understanding, defining, and solving of medical and biological problems.
- Specialize in helping to develop the artificial lung, magnetic resonance imaging, respiratory and cardiac pacemakers, and plastic heart valves.
- Engaged in the analysis and testing of different materials to determine whether they will be accepted or rejected when used in the body in artificial organs and grafts.

ADDITIONAL SKILLS

- Fluent in Spanish
- Working knowledge of German, French, and Italian
- Familiar with current computer programs and numerous online research resources

REFERENCES

Available upon request

Patricia Allen, RRA

645 Green Street • Nashville, TN 37214 • (615) 555-8765 • P.Allen@xxx.com

Work History

2003–Present • Vanderbilt Children's Hospital, Nashville, TN

Medical Records Administrator

• Analyze patient data for processing insurance requests and hospital care programs.

• Supervise medical records clerks and transcriptionists.

• Implemented new system for retrieving medical records.

• Developed in-service program for medical records clerks.

• Developed policies for processing insurance requests.

• Evaluated hospital medical records system.

2002–2003

Nashville General Hospital at Meharry, Nashville, TN

Medical Records Administrator

• Assisted staff in evaluating efficiency of patient medical care.

• Analyzed patient health care programs.

• Supervised all medical records clerks.

Education

1998–2002 • Vanderbilt University, Nashville, TN

Bachelor of Science in Medical Records Administration

Courses

• Anatomy

• Medical Records Administration

• Statistics

• Disease Classification

• Medical Law

• Computer Science

• Medical Terminology

Certification

Registered Records Administrator, 2002

References Available Upon Request

JASON L. PEABODY, M.D., F.A.C.P.

Assistant Clinical Professor, Department of Dermatology
James R. Wright University School of Medicine

Work Address
Department of Dermatology
James R. Wright University School of Medicine
690 N. Holland Street
Lexington, KY 40292
(502) 555-9820

Home Address
8902 Douglas Drive
Lexington, KY 40292
(502) 555-8753
E-mail: drpeabody@xxx.com

COLLEGES AND UNIVERSITIES ATTENDED
B.A., Northwestern University, Evanston, IL—1975
M.D., Indiana University of Medicine, Indianapolis, IN—1979

UNIVERSITY OR HOSPITAL APPOINTMENTS
Rotating Intern, 1979–1980
University of Oregon Health Sciences Center, Portland, OR

Residency in Dermatology, 1980–1982
University of Oregon, Health Sciences Center, Portland, OR

Fellowship, Dermatology, 1982–1983
University of Oregon, Health Sciences Center, Portland, OR

Associate Professor of Medicine, 1983–1995
University of Oregon, Health Sciences Center, Portland, OR

Professor of Medicine, 1995–present
James R. Wright University School of Medicine, Lexington, KY

BOARD CERTIFICATION
American Board of Dermatology, 1982
American Board of Dermatopathology, 1984

LICENSURE
Kentucky (#5555555)
Washington (inactive)
Oregon (inactive)
Indiana (#55555555)

PROFESSIONAL SOCIETIES
American Academy of Dermatology
American Society of Dermatologic Surgery
American Medical Association
American Society of Dermatopathology

COMMITTEES
Portland, OR
Residency Review Committee, 1981–1982
Pharmacy Committee, 1981–1982
Research and Development Safety Subcommittee, 1986
Private Practice Plan, 1987
Research, 1989
HMO-PPO Liaison Committee, 1992
Clinical Computing, 1993

Lexington, KY
Steering, Medical Outcomes, 1996
Residency Evaluation Committee, 1997

ELECTED NATIONAL POSITIONS
American Academy of Dermatopathology Board of Directors, 1992–1995,
    1997–present
Chairman, Annual Scientific Assembly, 1993
Chair, Data Management Committee

GRANT SUPPORT
Medical Research Foundation of Oregon
Travenol Laboratory
Upjohn Pharmaceutical Company
James R. Wright University School of Medicine
Miles Laboratory
University of Oregon Department of Medicine

REFERENCES
Available on request

Jennifer MacFarland

419 Pierce Street

Ann Arbor, MI 48103

J.Macfarland@xxx.com

(734) 555-5739

Objective

To obtain a position as a pharmacist in a retail drugstore.

Education

University of Michigan, Ann Arbor, MI
Senior Honors Student/Department of Pharmacology
Degree Expected: June 2008

Experience

Teaching Assistant, August 2007 to Present
Pharmacology Department, University of Michigan

Assist professors with grading papers, basic research tasks, and tutoring students.

Part-Time Cashier, July 2006 to August 2007
Star Discount Store, Ann Arbor, MI

Developed excellent cash management and customer relations skills. Trained new hires.

Experience continued

Administrative Assistant, Summers 2004, 2005
Stevenson Electrical, Ann Arbor, MI

Assisted executives with document preparation, data entry, and general office duties.

Community Service

Volunteer, Summer 2006
Habitat for Humanity

Volunteer Tutor, Adult Literacy Program, 2005 to 2006
Michigan Public Libraries

References

Available on request

ALAN FREDERICK SMITH, M.D.

Associate in Medicine • Department of Nephrology
Co-Director of Dialysis Center, VA Hospital

Home Address   *Office Address*
8 Dunmore Court   Division of Nephrology, Box 3036
Durham, North Carolina 27713   Duke University Medical Center
Alan.Smith@xxx.com   Durham, North Carolina 27710
(919) 555-0918   (919) 555-5043

DEGREES

B.S., Biomath, Union College, Schenectady, New York, 2001
M.D., Duke University, Durham, North Carolina, 2005

EDUCATION

Duke University School of Medicine
Durham, North Carolina
Nephrology Fellowship, 2005–2007

RESEARCH EXPERIENCE

Duke University Medical Center, July 2007–Present
Department of Nephrology
Supervisor: Joseph P. Major, M.D.
Conducted clinical trials and basic lab research on metallic bone disease.

Durham VA Hospital, August 2005–April 2007
Duke University Medical Center
Renal Physiology Laboratory
Department of Medicine
Supervisors: Mark George, M.D., and Carl Kline, M.D.
Researched the relation of products of renal arachidonic acid metabolism
to mechanisms of cell injury and cell death.

RESEARCH EXPERIENCE *continued*

State University of New York, Albany, New York, Summer 2004
Department of Surgery
Supervisor: Richard Alden, M.D.
Five-year retrospective study of postoperative complications and failure rate of herniorrhaphy.

SPECIALTY

Board Certified Internal Medicine, 2007

LICENSURE

North Carolina License of Medicine #55555, 2007

RESEARCH SUPPORT

National Institutes of Health
Training Grant Research Award, 2006–2007

HONORS

- Graduated magna cum laude, Union College
- AOA Symposium Poster Presentation
- Assistant Chief Resident, Duke University Medical Center, April–June 2005
- Supervised the residency program at Durham Regional Hospital

References Available Upon Request

MONICA RODRIQUEZ
5092 Ashland Drive
Indianapolis, IN 46220
Work: (317) 555-8000
Cell: (317) 555-2989
E-mail: M.Rodriquez@xxx.com

EDUCATION
Undergraduate
Walsh College, Canton, Ohio
Bachelor of Arts, double major in biology and chemistry, 2000

Graduate
Indiana University, College of Medicine, Indianapolis, Indiana
Medical Doctor, 2004

Postgraduate
Indiana University Hospital, Indianapolis, Indiana
• Internal Medicine Internship, June 2004–June 2005
• Internal Medicine Residency, June 2005–June 2007
• Nephrology Fellowship, June 2007–Present

CREDENTIALS
• National Board of Medical Examiners Certificate
• State Medical License for Indiana, 2005
• American Board of Internal Medicine, 2007

GRANTS
National Kidney Foundation of Indiana Affiliate, 2007–2008:
"Mechanisms of Glomerular Injury: Lipid-Induced Production of
Monocyte Chemotactic Factor by Cultured Mesangial Cells"

ACADEMIC HONORS AND AWARDS

Valedictorian, Walsh College, G.P.A. 4.0
Walsh College Academic Scholarship

Three Walsh College Honors Certificates

- Outstanding Junior Chemist in Akron section of the American Chemical Society
- Letter of Commendation in Internal Medicine
- Letter of Honors in Family Medicine

ASSOCIATIONS

- American Medical Association
- Indiana Medical Association

RESEARCH

Compiled drug elution timetables with capillary gas chromatographs at Accutox Toxicology Laboratory, 1999–2000.

REFERENCES AVAILABLE

PETER JOSEPH LITTLE

354 Long Hill Road • Middletown, CT 06457
(203) 555-9998 • Peter.Little@xxx.net

OBJECTIVE

Seeking a rewarding and challenging position in medical record administration where I can utilize over ten years of experience in the medical information field.

CAREER SUMMARY

Medical Record Technician, December 2005–Present
Johnson Memorial Hospital
• Led conversion from film imaging to digital imaging software and computers.
• Started introductory steps in replacing existing PC hardware in client base.
• Directed initial stages of development on new software module for insurance companies.
• Provided direction to all medical record clerks and medical record transcriptionists.

Medical Record Technician, January 2001–November 2005
Delta Community Hospital
• Responsible for analyzing records, cross-indexing medical information, and reviewing.
• Designed and implemented disease coding system.

Medical Record Clerk, August 1997–November 2000
Community North Hospital
• Entered codes in patient records, maintained registries, and gathered statistics on studies of bed utilization and operating room usage.

EDUCATION

National Technology Institute (Online University)
Associate's Degree, 1997
Medical Record Technician

REFERENCES AVAILABLE

TIUN LEUNG

School Address	*Home Address*
Duke University	345 Prospect Road
P.O. Box 55	Cleveland, OH 44136
Durham, NC 27706	T.Leung@xxx.com
(919) 555-9087	(419) 555-9064

CAREER OBJECTIVE

A position in biomedical engineering with emphasis on developing artificial organs and joints.

EDUCATION

Master of Science, Duke University, Durham, North Carolina
May 2007

Bachelor of Science, Duke University, Durham, North Carolina
May 2005

WORK EXPERIENCE

United Technologies, Edinburgh, IN
May 2006 to September 2006

- Tested artificial joint materials.
- Studied therapeutic devices.

Duke University Biomedical Laboratory, Durham, NC
August 2005 to May 2006

- Participated in labs analyzing synthetic organ tissues.
- Developed new strategies for producing synthetic materials.

HONORS AND ACTIVITIES

- Society of Women Engineers
- Phi Sigma Tau engineering sorority
- American Society of Biomedical Engineers

REFERENCES AVAILABLE

JANE P. WHITLOCK

5 MAPLE STREET

BUTTE, MONTANA 59701

(406) 555-7892

JANE.WHITLOCK@XXX.COM

JOB OBJECTIVE

To acquire a clinical position in a physical therapy facility emphasizing orthopedics and sports medicine, while continuing to develop my interest in occupational therapy.

EXPERIENCE

Memorial Hospital, 6/07–present

634-bed acute care facility

• As staff therapist, responsible for managing outpatient department.

• Worked closely with a neurosurgeon in developing an exercise program for post-op patients.

Nappanee Hospital, 7/03–6/07

254-bed acute care facility

• Responsible for inpatient and outpatient physical therapy care.

• Participated in a sports medicine clinic.

• Handled burn and multiple-trauma patients.

EDUCATION

University of Montana–Missoula

School of Physical Therapy and Rehabilitation Science

Bachelor of Science in Physical Therapy, 2003

PROFESSIONAL ORGANIZATIONS

Member, American Physical Therapy Association

REFERENCES

Available upon request.

✣ SUSAN MARIE COOPER

111 Central Avenue
Portland, OR 97202
Home: (503) 555-9087
Cellular: (503) 555-6477
Susie.Cooper@xxx.com

✣ EMPLOYMENT

Staff Occupational Therapist, Registered
3/07–Present
Occupational Therapy Department
Portland Hand Center
Portland, OR

Staff Occupational Therapist
1/04–3/07
Occupational Therapy Department
St. Joseph Medical Center
Portland, OR

Occupational Therapy Assistant
6/01–1/04
Occupational Therapy Department
Gresham Memorial Hospital
Gresham, OR

Page 1 of 2

✣ EDUCATION

Pacific University, 2001
Bachelor of Science
Occupational Therapy
Forest Grove, OR

✣ SPECIAL PROJECTS

Private Practice: Pediatrics, Independent Study

✣ AFFILIATIONS

American Occupational Therapy Association
Oregon Occupational Therapy Association

✣ REFERENCES

Available upon request

GORDON A. ROSIN

Major, United States Army • 5711 Norman Ave.
Fort Worth, TX 76103 • G.Rosin@xxx.com

PRESENT POSITION

Assistant Chief Nurse Anesthetist
Bradley Army Community Hospital, Fort Worth, TX
2006–present

EDUCATION

Troy State University, Troy, AL
B.S.N., 1995

Texas Wesleyan University, Fort Worth, TX
M.S., 2002

MILITARY EDUCATION

Clinical Specialist Course 91C • Army Medical Department
William Beaumont Army Medical Center, El Paso, TX
1997

Medical Field Service School
Academy of Health Sciences, Fort Sam, Houston, TX
1998

AMEDD Officers Advanced Course E-23
Academy of Health Sciences, Fort Sam, Houston, TX
2000

Combined Officers Advanced Staff Services School
Fort Leavenworth, KS
2001

MILITARY EDUCATION *continued*

School of Anesthesiology for Army Nurse Corps Officers, Phase I
Academy of Health Sciences, Fort Sam, Houston, TX
2002

School of Anesthesiology for Army Nurse Corps Officers, Phase II
Academy of Health Sciences, Fort Sam, Houston, TX
2003

AMEDD Officers Clinical Head Nurse Course
Academy of Health Sciences, Fort Sam, Houston, TX
2003

FORMER POSITIONS

Staff Nurse, Ortho/ICU, Part-Time
Jackson Hospital, Montgomery, AL • 1997–2000

Obstetric Anesthesia, Part-Time
Sierra Medical Center, El Paso, TX • 2000–2002

Obstetric Anesthesia, Part-Time
Vista Hills Medical Center, El Paso, TX • 2002–2004

Staff Nurse Anesthetist
William Beaumont Army Medical Center, El Paso, TX • 2004–2006

LICENSES

Registered Nurse, Alabama, 1995, #5-55555
Registered Nurse, Texas, 2002, #555555
Certified Registered Nurse Anesthetist, Texas, 2004, #5555
American Association of Nurse Anesthetists, 2005
Registered Nurse, Indiana, 2006, #55555555

REFERENCES AVAILABLE ON REQUEST

SUKI YOKASHIMA

5595 West Scott Street • Salt Lake City, UT 84112

Email: S.Yokashima@xxx.com

Home: (801) 555-8972

Cell: (801) 555-0988

JOB OBJECTIVE

To work in a neonatal nursery as a clinical specialist involved in the support of infants and children

EDUCATION

Bachelor of Science in Nursing, 2005
University of Utah, Salt Lake City, UT
Graduated with honors

EXPERIENCE

Wishard Hospital, Salt Lake City, UT
June 2005 to present
Staff nurse in the neonatal intensive care unit

AFFILIATIONS

Utah Nurses Association
National Association of Neonatal Nurses

REFERENCES

On request

Robert Jaurez

3897 Washington Blvd.

Tucson, AZ 85701

Bob.Jaurez@xxx.com

(520) 555-3467

Career Goal

To obtain a position as a medical illustrator.

Education

M.A., Medical Illustration in Art
September 2005–June 2008
University of San Diego, San Diego, CA
GPA 3.74
Courses included drawing, layout, photography, illustration techniques, zoology, physiology, chemistry, biology, and histology.

B.S., Zoology
September 2000–June 2005
University of Arizona, Tucson, AZ
Overall GPA 3.53
Major GPA 3.8
Undergraduate courses included a strong concentration of science with an emphasis on art.

Experience

Yuma Topic daily newspaper
Yuma, AZ
2000–2005 (summers)
Worked in the illustration department at a variety of tasks and in the layout design department.

References

Available upon request.

Yossif Patinkin, M.D.

114 Laurel Lane • Jamestown, PA 15904

Y.Patinkin@xxx.com • (314) 555-7874

Present Project

Private practice in family medicine with special interest in critical care management.

Background

7/05 to 9/08

Fellow, Department of Critical Care Medicine

Community Hospital, Pittsburgh, PA

10/03 to 6/05

Fellow, Department of Family Medicine

Temple University Hospital, Philadelphia, PA

7/02 to 9/03

Resident, PGY III Internal Medicine

Valley Memorial Hospital, Jamestown, PA

7/01 to 7/02

Resident, PGY II Internal Medicine

Valley Memorial Hospital, Jamestown, PA

7/00 to 6/01

Resident, PGY I Internal Medicine

Valley Memorial Hospital, Jamestown, PA

Background *continued*

5/00 to 6/00

Assistant Resident, Internal Medicine

Valley Memorial Hospital, Jamestown, PA

7/99 to 1/00

Attended the Stanley Kaplan Educational Center, Houston, TX

Undertook an extensive self-guided study of basic and clinical sciences.

7/98 to 6/99

Rotating Resident Internship

Brown Memorial Hospital, Dallas, TX

9/93 to 5/98

Bachelor of Medicine and Bachelor of Surgery

Christian Medical College, Dallas, TX

Affiliations

Associate Member, American College of Physicians

Licensure

Commonwealth of Pennsylvania, MD-55555555-L, DEA-55555555

Board certified in internal medicine by American Board of Internal Medicine, 9/03

Board eligible in family medicine by American Board of Internal Medicine

Board eligible in critical care medicine

References

Available on request

JENNIFER BAUER

93 WEST FOURTH STREET

LONG BEACH, CA 90808

E-MAIL: JENNY.BAUER@XXX.COM

HOME: (213) 555-9876

EDUCATION

Bachelor of Science in Cytotechnology, June 2006, GPA 3.65
California Institute of Technology, Pasadena, California
Dean's Honor List—six semesters

Relevant Courses:

Bacteriology

Physiology

Anatomy

Histology

Embryology

Zoology

Genetics

Chemistry

Computer classes

WORK EXPERIENCE

Cytotechnologist, June 2006–present
Circle Center Research Laboratory, Culver City, CA

Duties include identifying cell specimens collected by fine needle
aspiration and reporting findings to the pathologist. Use computers to
measure cells, a new technique that is being developed at Circle Center
Research Laboratory.

CERTIFICATION

The International Academy of Cytology
National Certification Agency for Medical Laboratory Personnel

REFERENCES

Available on request

Rita Garden

32 Elliott Avenue
Austin, Texas 78731
Rita.Garden@xxx.com
(512) 555-5618

Career Objective

To become a regional administrator in a large nursing home corporation.

Employment Highlights

Seven years of experience in the administration of nursing homes in Austin, Texas. Acted as administrator in facilities ranging from 60 to 175 beds, and in intermediate and skilled-care nursing homes.

Experience

2004–Present
Desert Valley Home, Austin Nursing Homes, Incorporated; Austin, Texas
Administrator

2003–2004
Austin Convalescent Hospital (Alzheimer's Unit), Goodwin Nursing Homes, Incorporated; Austin, Texas
Administrator

2001–2003
Southwest Nursing Home, Goodwin Nursing Homes, Incorporated; Austin, Texas
Began as Assistant Administrator, promoted to Administrator in 2002

Education

June 2001
B.S. in Health Science (summa cum laude)
University of Texas, Austin, Texas

Certification

June 2002
Nursing Home Administrator, License #5555

References on Request

ANN GOEBLE

666 Central Avenue • Raleigh, North Carolina 27601
A.Goeble@xxx.com • (919) 555-8972

JOB OBJECTIVE
To provide quality nutritional care to individuals in nursing homes.

EXPERIENCE
July 2007–Present
Consultant, Sunset Manor Nursing Home
Raleigh, NC
• Develop standards for nutritional care.
• Conduct routine clinical duties.
• Work as a team member with patients and physicians to build up undernourished patients.
• Developed a database detailing patients' specialized dietary needs.

June 1999–July 2007
Dietetic Assistant, Broadmoor Nursing Home
Starmount, NC
• Worked under dietetic supervisor in helping with menu planning, standardization of recipes, and the ordering of ingredients and supplies.
• Assisted patients with menu selections and wrote basic modified dietary plans for patients.

MEMBERSHIPS
American Dietetic Association
North Carolina Dietetic Association

EDUCATION
North Carolina State University
Raleigh, NC
1995–1999
B.S. in Dietetics

REFERENCES AVAILABLE UPON REQUEST

Michelle A. Harmon

339 Lexington Place • Iowa City, Iowa 52240

Home: (319) 555-8962 • Cellular: (319) 555-4329

E-mail: michelle.harmon@xxx.com

Objective

To work on a health and research team as a biomedical engineer

Education

Bachelor of Science, Biomedical Engineering
University of Iowa, Iowa City, IA
June 1998

Related Coursework

- Biomedical Engineering
- Biomedical Computers
- Engineering Biophysics
- Bioinstrumentation
- Biomechanics
- Biotransport
- Artificial Organs

Experience

Butler Williams Inc., Iowa City, Iowa
Bioengineer, 2003 to Present
Apply engineering principles to understanding the structure, function, and pathology of the human body. Use engineering concepts and technology to advance the understanding of biological, non-medical systems, such as maintaining and improving the quality of the environment and protecting human, animal, and plant life from toxicants and pollutants.

Affiliations

The International Certification Commission
American Society of Engineering Education

References

Available upon request

SCOTT M. FRANK, M.D.

983 Crestview Drive • Columbus, OH 43213 • (614) 555-9872 • scottfrank@xxx.com

EDUCATION

B.S., 1992
University of Cincinnati, Cincinnati, OH

M.D., 1997
University of Cincinnati, College of Medicine, Cincinnati, OH

POSTGRADUATE TRAINING

Residency, 1997–2000
East Virginia Graduate School of Medicine, Norfolk, VA

Fellow, Nephrology, 2000–2002
University of Iowa Hospitals and Clinics, Troy, IA

PROFESSIONAL EXPERIENCE

Private Practice in Nephrology, Dialysis, and Transplantation, 2002–Present
8978 Foxworth, Suite 555, Columbus, OH 43213

APPOINTMENTS

Medical Director of Dialysis, September 2006
Columbus Medical Center, Columbus, OH

Clinical Assistant Professor, Department of Internal Medicine, January 2006
Ohio State University Medical Center, Columbus, OH

COMMITTEES

Pharmacy and Therapeutics, Norfolk Medical Center, Norfolk, VA
Member, 1997–1999

Institutional Review Board
Cincinnati Medical Center
Member, 2003–2004

Capital Equipment
Iowa Medical Center
Member, 2001–Present

CERTIFICATIONS AND LICENSURE

Certification
American Board of Internal Medicine, 3/26/97, #55555
Nephrology, American Board of Internal Medicine, 11/11/97, #555555

Licensure (current)
Ohio, 7/2/97, #555555

REFERENCES

Available on request

Robin Peters

90 Pacific Coast Highway • Malibu, CA 90024 • (310) 555-3546 • Robin.Peters@xxx.com

Objective

To obtain a position with an ambulance company, hospital emergency room, or search-and-rescue team

Education

Sonoma State University, Rohnert Park, CA
B.A., Environmental Studies, January 2005
Included coursework in Advanced First Aid, Emergency Care, Physiology, and Psychology

Santa Rosa Junior College, Santa Rosa, CA
Emergency Medical Technician Course 1A
Fire Service/Auto Extrication, December 2005

Experience

Sonoma Life Support, Sonoma, CA, November 2005
Assisted paramedics and other EMTs on an ambulance as part of EMT certification

Emergency Room, Santa Rosa Hospital, Santa Rosa, CA, October 2005
Helped doctors and nurses in patient care as part of EMT certification

Home Care Program, Sonoma, CA, 2004
Nurse assistant for the elderly

Marine Conservation Corps, San Rafael, CA, Summers 2001–2003
Acted as corps member and driver

Personal Qualifications

• Excellent knowledge of medical terms
• Calm in emergency situations
• Polite, helpful, and compassionate

License and Certificate

Red Cross Community CPR Certificate, 2005
Red Cross Advanced First Aid, 2003

Affiliations

National Parks Conservation Association
Sierra Club

References Available on Request

Latisha Brown

1419 Cedar Drive
Dayton, OH 45226
(513) 555-8754
Latisha.Brown@xxx.com

Qualifications:	Bachelor of Science in Pharmacy, 2007 School of Pharmacy, Dayton University, Dayton, OH
Special Award:	Merrell Dow Dayton School of Pharmacy's Annual Award for Excellence, 2006
Present Position:	Pharmacy Graduate Intern Program Dayton Community Hospital Dayton, OH
Experience:	Hooks Pharmacy, Summer Student Dayton, OH 10 weeks, 2007 Royal Hospital, Summer Student Dayton, OH Eight weeks, 2006 Ohio Drug, Saturday Staff Dayton, OH 2001–2006
Professional Interests:	Clinical Pharmacy
References:	Available on Request

Peggy Martin

580 East Main Street
Boston, MA 02169
Peg.Martin@xxx.com
(617) 555-7690

Education

Bachelor of Science, Pharmacy
University of Massachusetts, Boston, MA
2000

Experience

Gillian Griffiths Chemists Ltd., 2005–present
187 High Street, Boston, MA
• Pharmacist, 2007–present
• Assistant Manager (responsible for two stores), 2005–2007

Hilton Drug Company, 2000–2005
41 High Street
Boston, MA
• Manager, 2003–2005
• Relief Manager, 2001–2003
• Assistant Manager, 2000–2001

Additional Training

MRPTG courses including:
• Developing Management Skills
• Security in the Pharmacy
• First Aid

References

Available on request

✧ ROBERTA J. STEWART

34 King Crossing • Denver, CO 80203 • (303) 555-1566 • R.Stewart@xxx.com

✧ CAREER OBJECTIVE

A position in office management in a medical or dental clinic.

✧ EDUCATION

Denver Community College
Denver, CO • 2006
Completed courses in Word, Access, Excel, PowerPoint, Lotus Notes, Medical Office Management and Database Management.

Denver Technical College
Denver, CO • 1992
Completed Dental Assistant/Receptionist program.

✧ EXPERIENCE

Office Manager
Denver Dental Clinic, 1998–Present
124 Aspen Way, Denver, CO 80215
• Handle office payroll and all billing for three dentists.
• Manage insurance issues and forms.
• Keep appointment book.
• Developed database for patient records.

Receptionist
Dr. Leroy Atkins, 1993–1998
470 Rocky Mountain Drive, Boulder, CO 80217
• Kept appointment book and updated records.
• Greeted patients and made sure they were comfortable.

Dental Assistant
Dr. Thomas Marks, 1992–1993
85 Rocky Mountain Drive, Denver, CO 80217
• Assisted the dentist chairside and in the lab.
• Took x-rays.
• Prepared patients for oral surgery.

✧ *References available.*

ERIC M. JEFFERSON, M.D.

Office Address   Home Address
Martin Laboratory of Clinical Research   9802 Allen Lane
St. Ann's Hospital   Carmel, IN 46032
Indianapolis, IN 46202   Ejefferson@xxx.com
(317) 555-9871   (317) 555-8466

EDUCATION & TRAINING
B.S., 1986
Oregon State University, Corvallis, OR

M.S. (Biochemistry), 1988
University of Oregon Medical School, Eugene, OR

M.D. (cum laude), 1992
University of Oregon Medical School, Eugene, OR

- Internship (general medicine), July 1992–July 1995
- Residency (internal medicine), July 1996–July 1999
Indiana University Medical School, Indianapolis, IN

- Fellowship (medical oncology), July 1999–July 2001
- Fellowship (clinical pharmacology), July 2001–July 2003
National Cancer Institute, National Institute of Health, Pittsburgh, PA

ACADEMIC APPOINTMENTS
- Clinical Pharmacologist, August 2004–present
Martin Laboratory for Clinical Research

- Assistant Professor of Medicine, September 2004–April 2006
- Assistant Professor of Pharmacology, February 2005–April 2007
- Associate Professor of Medicine, April 2006–present
- Associate Professor of Pharmacology, April 2007–present
Indiana University Medical School, Indianapolis, IN

CONSULTANTSHIPS
Consultant in Oncology
Indiana University Medical School

SPECIALTY BOARD STATUS
Diplomate, National Board of Medical Examiners
Cert. #555555, 1992

Diplomate, National Board of Medical Oncology
Cert. #555555, 1992

LICENSURE AND CERTIFICATION
State of Pennsylvania, #555-R, 1995
State of Indiana, #5555-L, 1995

PROFESSIONAL SOCIETIES
- Member, American Federation for Clinical Research
- Fellow, American College of Physicians
- Member, C. G. Hangley Institute of Bloomington

HONORS
- Phi Beta Sigma, 1985
- Phi Kappa Phi, 1986
- Alpha Omega Alpha, 1986

TEACHING ASSIGNMENTS DURING PAST TWO YEARS
Ward Attending Staff, Medicine Service, St. Ann's Hospital, one month per year
Duties included supervising and teaching of house staff and medical students on clinical clerkships and attending staff responsibility for medicine in-service patients.

Consultant in Oncology, St. Ann's Hospital, one month per year
Duties included supervising fellows in medical oncology, teaching senior medical students on elective rotation, and formulating treatment plans for inpatients with cancer. Fellowship mentor in clinical pharmacology and medical oncology.

PROFESSIONAL ACTIVITIES
Martin Laboratory for Clinical Research Committee Assignments:
- Oncology Action Group (new oncolytics selection)
- Oncology Strategy Working Group

SERVICES
Four-year member, Biostatistics Study and Planning Committee of Indiana University (Dr. June Reasonor, chair).

—Approximately 10 percent of time on the job spent as responsible physician in charge of the oncology patients in the Martin Clinic Service at St. Ann's Hospital. Duties include direct primary patient care of five to ten cancer patients in advanced states of disease. Twelve months of the year.

—April 1997, participated in an intensive one-week medical mission to the rural people of Haiti, sponsored by the national organization Lifeline and the Northside Christian Church of Indianapolis.

REFERENCES AVAILABLE ON REQUEST

ROSEMARIE JOHNSON

232 Lee Street

Durham, NC 27707

(919) 555-6541

R.Johnson@xxx.com

OBJECTIVE

To become a member of the medical staff in a small clinic.

EXPERIENCE

Registered Nurse

Durham Blood Bank, Durham, NC

2004 to present

- Draw blood, work with autologous program, and take charge of
  unit when supervisor is absent.

Private Duty Nurse

The Beck Agency, Durham, NC

2001 to 2004

- Provided long-term care in private homes.

Floor Nurse

Durham General Hospital, Durham, NC

2000 to 2001

- Floor nurse in premature delivery ward.

EDUCATION

Bachelor of Science in Nursing, University of North Carolina, Chapel Hill, 1999

Refresher Courses, Durham General Hospital, 1999 to 2007

- Care of Premature Infants
- Infant Nutrition
- Behavior Modification
- Addictive Behaviors

CERTIFICATION

Certified as Registered Nurse, North Carolina, 2004

REFERENCES FURNISHED ON REQUEST

Peter Simmons

678 Park Street

Portland, OR 97281

(503) 555-4527

Pete.Simmons@xxx.com

Objective

To obtain an executive position in marketing with a major pharmaceutical company dedicated to the research and development of new drugs.

Experience

5/05 to Present

Coast Pharmaceuticals, Portland, OR

• Design marketing strategies for local and national markets.

• Improved company's sales by over 15 percent during the last year.

• Developed successful marketing program for generic drugs.

1/04 to 5/05

Crestmore Laboratories, New York, NY

• Set regional sales record in six months.

• Exceeded company goals for the 2004 fiscal year.

• Developed sales marketing program for the northwest region.

Education

2003

M.B.A., UCLA, with concentration in marketing

Dean's List for six quarters

2001

B.A. in Business, University of Oregon, Eugene, OR

G.P.A. was 3.8/4.0

References Available

MARIA SANCHEZ

285 Spruce Street

Pittsburgh, PA 19103

Maria.Sanchez@xxx.com

(412) 555-7896

Experience

Full-Time Nursing Assistant, 6/06 to Present

Water's Edge Convalescent Hospital, Pittsburgh, PA

• Formulate care plans for patients.

• Administer medication.

• Assist with patients' personal needs.

• Take blood pressure and temperature, check respiration rates.

Part-Time Student in Nursing Assistant Program, 9/04 to 6/06

Mercy Hospital, Pittsburgh, PA

• Assisted in bathing, feeding, and diapering patients.

• Checked on patients and reported back to Nursing Assistants.

Teacher, 9/00 to 5/04

Douglas MacArthur High School, Manila, Philippines

• Taught English and reading programs.

License

Certified Nurse Assistant, 2006

Philadelphia, PA

References

Available on request

ANDREW FISHER

82 South 12th Street

Grand Rapids, MI 49503

(616) 555-2983

Andy.Fisher@xxx.com

- -

EXPERIENCE

My current position is medical record technician at the Hillside
Nursing Home, a 175-bed skilled care nursing facility in Grand
Rapids where I have worked for three years. My primary
responsibility is auditing medical records to make sure the staff has
carried out doctors' orders.

My previous job was at the Nimitz Navy Hospital in Detroit, where I
worked for two years as a medical record technician, putting
together patients' records after they left the hospital.

- -

EDUCATION

I graduated from Grand Rapids High School in the top 20 percent
of my class in 2003.

SKILLS

• Knowledgeable about current coding system regulations and any changes made by official agencies that affect coding information policies.

• Understand third-party reimbursement regulations, including payment procedures of health insurance firms and health maintenance organizations.

• Skilled eye for details, patterns, and discrepancies.

REFERENCES

Personal and professional references are available and will be furnished on request.

CHRISTINE K. ROCK

15 Albert Lane
Vancouver, British Columbia V5Y IV4
Canada
ckrock@xxx.com
(604) 555-8963

JOB OBJECTIVE
To use my pharmacy, communication, and organizational skills in a
challenging position as a hospital pharmacist.

QUALIFICATIONS
• Pharmacy degree (four-year)
• Advanced Resuscitation Award SSRL
• Award of Merit SSRL
• Duke of Edinburgh Award
• Completed third year of BSC honors

STANDARD/FURTHER EDUCATION
2004–2008
University of British Columbia
Vancouver, British Columbia
Bachelor of Science, Pharmacy

2000–2004
Victoria High School
Vancouver, British Columbia

Subjects Studied
• Fundamentals of Pharmacology
• Pharmaceutical Chemistry I–V
• Pharmacy Practice
• Biopharmaceutics and Drug Disposition
• Drugs and Disease
• General Practice of Pharmacy
• Statistics
• Pharmaceutics I

STANDARD/FURTHER EDUCATION *continued*

- Physiology I and II
- Physical Organic and Inorganic Chemistry
- Interpersonal Skills
- Bioscience
- Pharmaceutical Science and Drug Development
- Applications and Implications of Computers
- Marketing for Pharmacists

EXPERIENCE

July 2007–September 2007
Rupert Group Research Limited
- Assisted researchers in well-respected community pharmacy laboratory.
- Gained experience operating drug analysis equipment.

July 2006
Prince Edward Hospital
- Assigned to follow a tutor for a week, thus being involved in all aspects of hospital pharmacy.

June 2005–June 2007 (vacation and Saturday work)
Fraser Pharmacy
- Involved in all aspects of a community pharmacy.
- Dealt with customers at medicine and cosmetic counters.
- Prepared and endorsed prescriptions.

December 2004–June 2005
Vancouver Regional Council
Activity specialist (lifeguard) at a local youth club.
- Carried out safety precautions and instructed staff in the proper use of equipment.

June 2003–September 2003
Rosedale District Council
Lifeguard
- Supervised public swimming at an outdoor pool.

REFERENCES

Available upon request

Evan L. Waterfield

1254 Plaza Drive
Youngstown, OH 44512
Evan.Waterfield@xxx.com
(216) 555-8989

Education

June 2001 to January 2003
Ohio Vocational Schools, Inc.
Youngstown, OH
Completed practical nursing program.

Experience

Sleepy Hollow Nursing Home
45 Diamond Lane
Youngstown, OH 44513

Director of Staff Development, February 2005 to Present
Interview new patients and their families, review facility patient care plan and revise
when necessary, orient new staff, give in-service workshops for staff to update
knowledge of equipment, medicine, and changes in facility.

Staff Nurse, February 2003 to January 2005
Passed medicines, gave treatments, and provided basic nursing care.

License

Licensed Practical Nurse: Ohio license #5555

References

Available upon request

PETRA LEVENTHAL

109 Beach Drive • Virginia Beach, VA 23456 • (804) 555-9852 • P.Leventhal@xxx.com

OBJECTIVE

To secure a teaching position at a major medical school

WORK STYLE

- Specialist in resolving eating disorders
- Skilled in adapting counseling to client
- Analytic and versatile thinker
- Communicate with clients and parents with warmth and diplomacy

EXPERIENCE

Clinical Psychologist, 2004 to Present
Alta Vista Hospital, Virginia Beach, VA

- Established an eating disorder clinic
- Counseled over 100 teenagers with eating disorders
- Initiated peer counseling program
- Developed intern program
- Created a program to assess which clients would require hospitalization

Assistant Professor, 2003 to 2004 (academic year)
University of Virginia, Charlottesville, VA

- Taught class on eating disorders
- Received psychology department's "Excellence in Teaching Award"

EDUCATION

Ph.D. in Psychology, 2004
University of Virginia, Charlottesville, VA
Concentration: eating disorders

M.S. in Psychology, 2002
Yale University, New Haven, CT

B.A. in Psychology, 2000
Georgetown University, Washington, D.C.
Graduated magna cum laude

AFFILIATIONS

- Virginia Association of Psychologists, secretary
- American Association of Psychologists
- Eating Disorder Association of America

REFERENCES

Available on request

Victoria Marie Hooper

4687 Braewick Drive
Indianapolis, IN 46236
vicky_hooper@xxx.com
(317) 555-0963

Job Objective

Seeking a full-time position as a registered nurse with eventual entry into a management position.

Education

B.S., Nursing, 1995
Salve Regina College
Newport, RI

Skills and Abilities

Public Relations
• Chair/coordinator for several health fairs
• Health risk assessment coordinator
• Health-related counselor, providing health screening

Management
• Eleven years as navy nurse, managing subordinates including corps members and junior nurses
• Chair of hospital/nursing-related committees
• Charge nurse in multifaceted family practice clinic
• Dual role as nursing education/patient education coordinator

Work Experience

Health Nurse
Fort Benjamin Harrison Community Hospital
March 2007 to present

Nursing Education/Patient Education Coordinator
August 2005 to December 2006

Work Experience *continued*

Charge Nurse
August 2004 to August 2005
Family Practice Clinic

Staff Nurse: Medical-Surgical
June 2004 to August 2004
Orlando Naval Hospital

Staff Nurse: Pediatric Acute Care Clinic
November 2002 to June 2004
Portsmouth Navy Hospital

Charge Nurse: Pediatrics
March 1999 to November 2002
Jacksonville Naval Hospital

Staff Nurse: Orthopedics, Pediatrics, and ICU/RR
December 1995 to February 1999
Great Lakes Naval Hospital

Military Service

November 1995
Commissioned
United States Navy Nurse Corps

December 2006
Honorable Discharge from United States Navy

References Available

Mario Jones

80 Chestnut Street

Minneapolis, MN 55416

Email: Mario.Jones@xxx.com

Home: (612) 555-8461

Cell: (612) 555-3932

Physical Therapy License

Minnesota #55555

Employment Experience

August 2000 to Present

Co-owner of Physical Therapy Associates of St. Louis Park

St. Louis Park, MN

Specializing in outpatient neurological and orthopedic diagnoses

October 1998 to August 2000

Acute Rehabilitation Staff Therapist

Bloomington Memorial Hospital

Bloomington, MN

August 1996 to October 1998

Physical Therapy Aide

Minneapolis Rehabilitation Center

Minneapolis, MN

August 1994 to August 1996

Physical Therapy Aide

Crestwood Rehabilitation Hospital

Rochester, MN

Professional Education

B.S. Degree in Physical Therapy, 1993
University of California, Santa Barbara

B.A. Degree in Pre-Physical Therapy, minor in Psychology, 1991
California State University, Turlock

Continuing Education

December 2006
Cranio-Sacral I

October 2005
The Active Foot Symposium

February 2005
New Treatments for Lower Back Pain

May 2004 to November 2004
Myofascial Strategies II

October 2003 to April 2004
Myofascial Strategies I

October 1999
Traumatic Brain Injury Conference

April 1999
NDT for Adult Hemiplegia Certification Course

References Available

MARK JOHNSON

971 Gable Street • Boca Raton, FL 33431

(407) 555-8765 • M.Johnson@xxx.com

WORK HISTORY

2006–present

Clear Speech

Boca Raton, FL

Speech-language pathologist

• Evaluation, diagnosis, and treatment of children with speech disorders.

2005–2006

Santa Clara County School for the Deaf

San Jose, CA

Speech-language pathologist and sign language instructor

• Taught students and family the fundamentals of sign language.

2004–2005

Private Practice

San Jose, CA

• Specialized in screening of preschoolers for early identification of hearing- and speech-impaired students.

2001–2004

San Jose Public Schools

San Jose, CA

Speech-language pathologist

• Elementary school district: Early identification of hearing and speech impaired.

• High school district: Treatment of mentally and physically impaired students with speech problems and learning disabled students with ESL.

EDUCATION

2001
Northwestern University
Evanston, IL
M.A., Speech Pathology

1999
University of Wisconsin
Madison, WI
B.A., Arts and Sciences with Speech and Hearing specialty

CERTIFICATION

Certificate of Clinical Competence of the American Speech and Hearing
Association

PROFESSIONAL AFFILIATIONS

• American Speech and Hearing Association
• Florida Speech and Hearing Association
• Greater Boca Raton Speech and Hearing Association

SPECIAL QUALIFICATIONS

Fluent at signing

REFERENCES

Available on request

RICHARD A. LAGNER, M.D.

5677 N. Senate Avenue, Suite 561 • Bethesda, Maryland 20811

Home: (301) 555-3354 • Cellular: (301) 555-8891

Email: Dick.Lagner@xxx.com

MILITARY SERVICE
United States Navy
Rank: Commander
June 1990–July 2001

EDUCATION AND TRAINING
Premedical
B.A., Notre Dame University
South Bend, Indiana
1984–1986

Medical School
M.D., Indiana University
Indianapolis, Indiana
1987–1990

Internship
Surgical Internship
National Naval Medical Center
Bethesda, Maryland
1990–1991

Residency
General Surgery
Naval Regional Medical Center
Portsmouth, Virginia
1991–1995

Plastic Surgery
National Naval Medical Center
Bethesda, Maryland
1995–1997

BOARD CERTIFICATION
American Board of Plastics and Reconstructive Surgery, 2005

TEACHING POSITIONS
Assistant Clinical Professor
Microvascular Surgery Techniques
Naval Regional Medical Center
Portsmouth, Virginia
October 2003

Instructor, Hyperbaric Oxygen Therapy
Memorial Medical Center
Long Beach, California
March 2004

Instructor, Liposuction Techniques
Midwestern Regional Lipoplasty Symposium
Minneapolis, Minnesota
May 2006

MEMBERSHIPS
- International Microsurgical Society
- American Burn Association
- American Association of Tissue Banks
- American Medical Association
- Diplomate, American Board of Plastic Surgery

DIRECTORSHIPS/CHAIRMANSHIPS
Consultant, Hyperbaric Oxygen Therapy
Memorial Medical Center, 2005–present

Consultant, Tissue Bank
Central Minnesota Blood Center, 2005–2006

Burn Director
Memorial Medical Center, 2007–present

REFERENCES AVAILABLE

PAM T. PHILLIPS

444 Mulberry Street
Jackson, MS 39216
(601) 555-7624
pamela.phillips@xxx.com

JOB OBJECTIVE

To work in a neonatal nursery as a specialist in clinical care, and to prepare parents to provide the care their babies will need when released from the hospital.

EDUCATION

University of Mississippi Medical Center, 2005
Jackson, MS
Master of Science in Nursing with a minor in education

University of Mississippi Medical Center, 2002
Jackson, MS
Bachelor of Science in Nursing

WORK EXPERIENCE

Providence Children's Hospital, 2005 to Present
Jackson, MS
Position: Staff Nurse
• Create and execute media presentations for parents of special care infants.
• Perform special nursing skills associated with caring for intensive care infants.

University of Michigan Medical Center, 2002 to 2005
Jackson, MS
Position: Staff Nurse
• Devised new organizational structure to accommodate expanded ward.
• Acted as role model for new trainees receiving on-the-job training.

REFERENCES

Available upon request.

Chapter 6

Sample Cover Letters

This chapter contains sample cover letters for people pursuing a wide variety of jobs and careers.

There are many different styles of cover letters in terms of layout, level of formality, and presentation of information. These samples also represent people with varying amounts of education and work experience. Choose one cover letter or borrow elements from several different cover letters to help you construct your own.

January 14, 20—

MARTIN A. GORDON
1090 Oak Drive
Madison, WI 54702

Mercy Hospital
6225 Maple Drive
Madison, WI 54702

To Whom It May Concern:

This letter is in response to the advertisement for an emergency medical technician that appeared in the *Daily Cardinal* last Friday evening. Please accept my resume in consideration for this position.

With a degree from the University of Wisconsin and five years of work experience as a medical technician at Community North Hospital in Madison, Wisconsin, I believe that I am suited to your hospital's needs.

Thank you for your time and consideration. I look forward to hearing from you soon.

Sincerely,

Martin A. Gordon
(608) 555-8954

Enclosure

January 27, 20—

Sanji Kumar
2556 Forest Street
Houston, TX 77063

Personnel Director
Valley Hospital
P.O. Box 228964
Birmingham, AL 35222-8964

Dear Personnel Director:

Please consider my application for a position as a dietitian. I graduated from Purdue University with a Bachelor of Science degree in Dietetics. I have been a registered dietitian for the past three years.

I feel that my experience as a dietitian in a nursing home and clinic, along with my education, qualifies me for a position with Valley Hospital. I will continue to be successful as a dietitian because I enjoy the challenge of helping people regain their health through proper diet. Furthermore, I work hard and am concerned with doing my best at all times.

I would like to have an interview to discuss how my placement with your hospital would benefit both of us. Please phone me anytime at (713) 555-8866. I look forward to hearing from you.

Yours truly,

Sanji Kumar

Enclosure

Katherine Malloy

510 Pine Street • San Ramon, CA 94542 • (510) 555-5642

Kathy.Malloy@xxx.com

February 8, 20—

Dr. Elena Rodriguez
50 Central Avenue
Danville, CA 94526

Dear Dr. Rodriguez:

Thank you for speaking with me yesterday about the dental hygienist opening in your office. After talking with you and learning more about your office and philosophy, I feel more confident than ever that my skills would benefit you and your staff. With my extensive experience and outstanding education and training, I believe that I would be an asset to your office.

I am enclosing a copy of my resume to give you a better idea of my employment history and would appreciate the opportunity to discuss it further with you in person.

Thank you for your time and consideration, and I look forward to hearing from you at your convenience.

Sincerely,

Katherine Malloy

Enclosure

March 25, 20—

Dorothea P. Russell

209 East Main Street

Philadelphia, PA 19103

(215) 555-9845

Saint Vincent's Hospital

635 Medical Drive, Suite 248

Wilkes-Barre, PA 18711

Dear Sir/Madam:

I am interested in the position of psychiatric social worker, which you advertised in this Sunday's *Citizen Voice*. As you can see from the enclosed resume, I have considerable experience working with adult psychiatric patients in a variety of mental health care facilities, including the traditional hospital setting.

I would like the opportunity to meet with you to discuss my qualifications. I think that I would be a productive addition to your hospital staff.

Sincerely,

Dorothea P. Russell

Enclosure

Margaret Morgan

3033 Diamond Drive • Indianapolis, IN 46220

317-555-1881 • mmorgan@xxx.com

November 8, 20—

Riley Children's Hospital
5892 Dupont Avenue
Indianapolis, IN 46256

Dear Sir/Madam:

I am responding to your ad in the *Indiana Times* for a neonatology instructor.

I am presently a graduate student at the Indiana University School of Nursing, pursuing an advanced degree in Pediatric Nursing Education. I plan to graduate in June of next year with honors.

My resume is enclosed for your review. As you can see, I have extensive experience in the field of education and have further expanded my credentials to include specialization in the area of neonatology.

Riley Children's Hospital is the kind of well-respected and venerable institution that attracts me. The focus on patient care and well-being, in particular, is in alignment with my personal work philosophy. I believe strongly that my skills would be of benefit to Riley Children's Hospital.

Please contact me if you require additional information. I look forward to hearing from you.

Sincerely,

Margaret Morgan

February 8, 20—

Anthony H. Cohen
167 Tuxedo Drive
Redding, CT 06896
(203) 555-1678

Mr. George Smart
Director of Personnel
Vocational Technical College
8775 West Douglas Street
Virginia Beach, VA 23456

Dear Mr. Smart:

For the past ten years, I have had a rewarding career with Central State Hospital in Connecticut. I now find myself ready to take on a new challenge as a teacher of mental health workers.

During my career at Central State Hospital, I have held positions as mental health counselor and director of psychiatric social work. Being part of the mental health community has shown me the great need for well-trained, motivated, and dedicated workers in this area.

I would like the opportunity to speak with you about my background and the potential areas where my expertise can be used to train mental health workers. The enclosed resume describes my qualifications.

I will call early next week to discuss your current needs and the possibility of meeting with you in person.

Sincerely yours,

Anthony H. Cohen

August 27, 20—

Michael K. Smith
2234 Eden Hollow Road, Suite 5
New York, NY 10020
Office: (212) 555-7788
Home: (212) 555-0098

Mr. John Boyd
The Far West Pharmaceutical Company
7722 Oakwood Drive
San Ramon, CA 94527

Dear Mr. Boyd:

After researching the Far West Pharmaceutical Company, what I learned about its progressive and innovative nature really appealed to me. I think that our approach and needs coincide and could be a great match.

I am looking for a position as a salesperson with a pharmaceutical house after spending the past five years as a pharmacist in a retail store. My enclosed resume describes my experience and qualifications since my graduation from college.

I look forward to hearing from you soon to set up an appointment for an interview. Please keep all contact personal and confidential.

Sincerely,

Michael K. Smith

Enclosure

David Allen Wong

5578 Douglas Drive • Council Bluffs, Iowa 51504 • david.wong@xxx.com

---

October 19, 20—

Human Resources
Green Glen Assisted Living
825 North Woodland Drive
Council Bluffs, Iowa 51503

To Whom It May Concern:

I am writing to inquire about any openings you may have for clinical nurse specialists in geriatric medicine. My experience in geriatric nursing includes working in the Alzheimer's unit of Memorial Hospital and the Oak Brook Nursing Home. Recently, I completed a Gerontological Nurse Practitioner training program. In addition, I hold gerontology certification.

If you should have an interest in further discussing my qualifications, please contact me at (712) 555-0134.

My resume is enclosed for your review.

Sincerely,

David Allen Wong

Enclosure

October 8, 20—

Charles D. Stiles

6225 High Drive
New Brunswick, NJ 08901
(201) 555-2609

Human Resources Department
Clear Laboratories
13 Aspen Drive
Trenton, NJ 06902

Dear Sir/Madam:

I am writing to you with the hope that you might have an opening soon in your laboratory for a medical technologist. If you do not, I would appreciate you keeping my resume on file for future opportunities.

I recently completed course work at Johns Hopkins for a master's degree in medical technology. Presently, I am completing my research project in microbiology.

I am a sincere, hardworking individual with the ability to learn quickly. I enjoy challenging work and am capable of performing under pressure.

Thank you for taking the time to consider my qualifications and candidacy. I look forward to hearing from you soon.

Sincerely yours,

Charles D. Stiles

Enclosure

January 19, 20—

Maria Monzon

3345 Lucas Street

Dallas, TX 75235

m.monzon@xxx.com

Personnel Director

Washington Township School Corporation

93 Lindenwood Ave.

Austin, TX 78768

Dear Personnel Director:

I am writing to obtain further information regarding employment with your school corporation as a school nurse. I recently read about your corporation in the *Texan State Journal* and would like to inquire about career opportunities within your school district.

I will be graduating from Southern Methodist University in May with a Bachelor of Science degree in Nursing. Throughout my collegiate career, I have maintained a balanced schedule of activities and academics. In addition, my summer internship provided invaluable work experience in the emergency room at Kennedy Hospital.

A copy of my resume is enclosed for your review. If you need further information, I will be more than happy to provide you with the necessary materials.

I know how busy you must be during this time of year, but I would appreciate a few minutes of your time. I may be reached at the above address or by calling (214) 555-2203. I look forward to hearing from you regarding my future with your school corporation.

Sincerely,

Maria Monzon

Enclosure: Resume

Jerome Palmer
5544 Wildwood Drive
Westlake, Ohio 44145
(614) 555-4014

December 17, 20—

Ruth Fong
Pacific Press
255 Long Hill Rd.
Middletown, CT 06457

Dear Ms. Fong:

I wish to apply for a position as a medical illustrator with Pacific Press.

I hold an undergraduate degree in biology and a master's degree in medical illustration. In addition, I am a member of the Association of Medical Illustrators. I have an extensive and varied background working on ophthalmology drawings and working with educators and authors. This experience, combined with my schooling and personal interest in illustrating, could be very valuable to your company. Also, I would be willing to relocate for a position with Pacific Press.

Enclosed is my resume for your reference. Please feel free to call me and set up an interview at your convenience.

Sincerely,

Jerome Palmer

January 23, 20—

STEPHANIE KOHL

3412 South York Avenue

Chicago, IL 61646

213-555-6321

Crystal Brown

250 Marquette Avenue

Minneapolis, MN 55401

Dear Ms. Brown:

I am seeking a position as a speech-language pathologist in an elementary-school setting, as I am eagerly planning to relocate to the greater Minneapolis area.

I received my master's degree in speech-language pathology from the University of Minnesota and hold state licenses in Illinois and Minnesota. My experience includes working in public elementary and secondary schools as well as at a county school for the hearing-impaired. In addition, I sign fluently.

My resume is enclosed to assist you in evaluating my qualifications. If you need further information, please contact me.

I look forward to meeting with you to discuss your current staffing needs and how my knowledge and skills would enhance your school district. Thank you for your consideration.

Sincerely,

Stephanie Kohl

Enclosure

November 21, 20—

Kathy Johnson

1516 North Central Avenue

Syracuse, NY 13057

(315) 555-3953

Dr. James Day

Clay Hospital

9888 West Washington Blvd.

Syracuse, NY 13057

Dear Dr. Day:

This letter is in reply to your advertisement in the *Syracuse Star* on Sunday, November 19, seeking a music therapist. I believe I am an excellent candidate for that position.

I earned a degree in music therapy from Syracuse University in May of this year. Recently, I completed an internship at Coleman Hospital in Saratoga Springs, where I worked with severely disabled children. I play the piano, guitar, violin, and recorder and enjoy using folk music as a part of my treatment therapy. I have attached a qualifications summary and other pertinent data for your consideration.

I think that Clay Hospital can utilize my experience and qualifications, and I look forward to an interview with you.

Sincerely,

Kathy Johnson

Enclosure

March 13, 20—

Jill R. McCoy
473 Hill Drive West
Lincolnwood, IL 60646
(847) 555-6320

Ms. Julia Serafini
Crestwood Manor
6341 Crestwood Dr.
Naperville, IL 60565

Dear Ms. Serafini:

I will be graduating from Northwestern University in May. I am seeking a position as an occupational therapist in a nursing home setting.

My education at Northwestern University exposed me to the latest developments in occupational therapy. It also provided me with the opportunity to work with individuals in retirement communities, senior citizen centers, and rehabilitation centers. In addition, I have enhanced my education with extra courses in gerontology.

Enclosed, you will find my resume. A complete credentials file is available upon request through Northwestern University, Educational Placement Office; 4600 S. Main Street; Evanston, IL 60043; (847) 555-9987.

I would like to request an interview with Crestwood Manor. I may be contacted at the above number.

Sincerely,

Jill R. McCoy

Enclosure

January 8, 20—

❖ ELIZABETH A. GROSSA

1346 E. 22nd St. #105
Chicago, IL 60302
(312) 555-9862

Optics Plus
8465 Baker Street
Sweetwater, TN 88485

To Whom It May Concern:

This letter is in response to the Optics Plus ad placed in the *Sweetwater Press* last Sunday.

I have a Master in Ophthalmic Optics certificate and hold a Tennessee license to dispense eyeglasses. I have worked in a hospital eye clinic for seven years and would now like to work in a retail optical store. Your ad was of particular interest to me as the job is for a position in the Sweetwater area.

My experience in the hospital environment has given me the opportunity to handle a wide variety of vision needs. Besides being a skilled optician, I have been told that my communication skills are excellent.

My resume is enclosed, detailing my work experience, certification, and educational background. I feel that my qualifications would be an asset to your corporation.

I would welcome the opportunity for a personal interview to discuss the position at Optics Plus.

Sincerely,

Elizabeth A. Grossa

December 4, 20—

George Long
655 Kelton Avenue
Los Angeles, CA 90024
(310) 555-9542

Anita Johnson
Los Angeles Drug Company
500 South Summit Drive
Burbank, CA 95123

Dear Ms. Johnson:

Please accept this letter as an application for the position of manager of the
prescription department in the Burbank branch of the Los Angeles Drug
Company. I have enclosed a copy of my resume for your review.

Through my present employment as a pharmacist with Goldman Drugs, I have
gained firsthand experience in merchandising, advertising, purchasing stock,
and supervising pharmacists and clerks. My formal education also includes an
undergraduate degree in business. Furthermore, I possess the interpersonal
skills and strong professional background that this position requires.

I would very much like to discuss my qualifications further in an interview.

Sincerely,

George Long

December 9, 20—

Joanne Powers
95 Lowell Drive
Kalamazoo, MI 49001
(616) 555-4889

Dr. Charlene Dixon
Kraft Medical Center
1000 Campus Drive
Kalamazoo, MI 49001

Dear Dr. Dixon:

I am responding to your advertisement in last Friday's *Gazette*. I am interested in a full-time position as a receptionist/secretary in your office.

Presently, I am working as a secretary in the office of Dr. Charles Williams, who will be retiring at the end of this month. My experience with Dr. Williams has included billing, data entry, patient scheduling, clerical work, and handling collection of patient accounts.

I am a self-starter who is resourceful, outgoing, efficient, service-oriented, and extremely organized. Superior recommendations are available from my current employer.

I look forward to hearing from you in the near future to schedule an interview.

Yours truly,

Joanne Powers

Enclosure

November 12, 20—

FRANCES MILLER
225 Landon Drive
Ionia, Michigan 49546
(616) 555-1053

Ralph Jansen, D.D.S.
1224 East Drive
Detroit, Michigan 48079

Dear Doctor Jansen,

Are you looking for someone who can:

• Play a key role in patient care?
• Work with children and adults in a gentle and caring manner?
• Effectively handle emergencies?
• Offer knowledge in areas such as dental implants and cosmetic bonding?
• Work on evenings and Saturdays?

In the ten years that I have worked as a dental assistant, I have assisted dentists in general dentistry as well as handled billing and appointments. In addition, I have experience with computer-aided dentistry. My experience has taught me the importance of good people skills and keeping abreast of the most recent technological advances in dentistry.

I look forward to the opportunity to meet with you personally to discuss my qualifications as a dental assistant. You may contact me in the evenings at the above telephone number.

Very truly yours,

Frances Miller

Enclosure

May 21, 20—

Michael R. Crowe
19 East 83rd Street, Apt. 32
New York, New York 10024
(212) 555-5626

Ms. Linda Lansing
Director, Human Resources
New York General Hospital
78 Lexington Avenue
New York, New York 10028

Dear Ms. Lansing:

Please accept this letter and my resume as an application for a position on the New York General Hospital staff. As a compassionate, hardworking professional who is willing to put in long hours, I believe I can make a positive contribution to your hospital.

As you may note in my resume, I have recently completed my residency at Walter Reed Hospital in Washington, D.C. During my time at Walter Reed, I also worked as a volunteer three nights a week for the Homeless Help Program. Through my volunteer activities, I have gained experience working with a vast number of individuals of various ages and socioeconomic backgrounds.

Besides solid medical skills, you will find that I have exceptionally strong organizational skills and am able to work independently with little or no supervision. I am looking for a hospital where I can best utilize my personal and professional skills and satisfy my desire to serve the community.

Should my qualifications meet the needs of your hospital, I would appreciate the opportunity for a personal interview at your earliest convenience. If you should need any additional information regarding my qualifications, please do not hesitate to contact me at any time.

Thank you for your time and consideration. I look forward to talking with you in the very near future.

Sincerely,

Michael R. Crowe

Enclosure: Resume, References